To Den

Best wishes &
Thank you.

Short Trips and Other Secrets

Eleanor (Ellie)

By
Eleanor Exum Elder Speer

ISBN 0-9701754-0-X

DEDICATIONS

To James E. Morton, Sr., without whom there wouldn't have been much to write about

and

To Niki, my initial inspiration;

and

To dear Leila for renewed inspiration.

BIOGRAPHICAL SKETCH
re
ELEANOR EXUM ELDER SPEER

A native of Plymouth, N. C., having spent the majority of her years in New York City, and presently residing in Jamaica, New York, she has always been a member of some church choir, always doing soprano solo work. She has appeared in several theatrical productions with the Rochdale Players in Queens County, including "South Pacific," "Mame,"and "Pajama Game," in which she played the leading role of "Babe." She also sang with the Carr-Hill Singers of Jamaica, N.Y. for several years as well as with the Clark Family Chorus which was based in the Bronx. She continues to sing on various choirs and at weddings and funerals.

She is a former Court Reporter, retired since 1989 from New York State Supreme Court. She began writing in 1976, describing her vacation trips for her mother who lived in North Carolina at the time. Several years later she discovered that her mother was passing her "letters" around town and, before she realized it, she had a request list of seniors and shut-ins from various parts of the country who wanted a copy of whatever she wrote. One senior in particular, who resides in Chicago, insisted that she must get published.

She does a lot of traveling with her travel mate Jim (sometimes referred to as Jem, his actual initials). But when not traveling or writing or singing, or dabbling in photography, you will find her at the bridge table, where she has attained the level of ruby.

* * *

TABLE OF CONTENTS

IS TO LAUGH

While on assignment from my job in New York City to work in Albany for two weeks, the first weekend found me without family or friends, so I accepted an invitation from a Jewish co-worker, also on assignmemt from New York City, to join her for dinner at her brother's home in Albany.

Although she was sure that I would be welcomed, I insisted that she call ahead, since I am black.

Upon arrival at her brother's home the entire family welcomed me, including their four-year-old son, who took a liking to me. And as I played with the child he said, "What's that?" indicating a very dark spot on the back of my right hand. I quickly replied, "Oh, I burned my hand." He stood off, stared at me and then said, "Gee, you must have burned yourself all over."

* * *

SOON COME

It was a cold 33 degrees outside at Kennedy International airport, and by 1 p.m. our jet was taxiing down the runway. At last! Saturday, December 18, 1965, and our party of **six was** heading for Montego Bay, Jamaica, West Indies.

Three and a half hours later we landed on "The Blessed Isle," where the weather was 86 degrees. At 4:30 p.m. the sun was still high in the sky and darkness did not fall until 6:30. We found it odd that although thousands of miles from New York there was no need to change our watches; we were still in the same time zone.

As our tiny red car (there were two other cars with us) drove away from the airport, the first sign we saw was "Remember to drive to the left." The narrow, two-lane road was beautifully landscaped with poinsettia and we were surrounded by lush greenery and rolling hills and mountains. The sky was an unbelievable blue and even the cloud formations seemed different from those back home.

First, we drove past the plush resort hotels and tourist homes and fancy shops, which soon gave way to the main street of Montego Bay. It looked like early Saturday evening in a small town just before Christmas, and so it was. The crowds were such that for a moment I thought we were in China, except for the fact the people were predominantly black instead of yellow. And we were struck by the signs of poverty which prevailed this crowded thoroughfare. It was a good feeling to have the protection of the car around us.

As the road lengthened, the crowds were left behind us and it became a narrow, snake-like mountain road that winded its way up and around the mountains, reaching such altitudes that the view from the car window seemed like a view from an airplane. It was quite beautiful and a bit frightening at the same time. Round and around we climbed, coming now and then to a straight, flat stretch and then back into what I called "the snake." The plane trip from New York to Montego Bay seemed very short compared to the 32 miles from MoBay, as the natives call it, to Savanna La Mar, where we were to stay. To our amazement we found that the road had more people than cars. It was beginning to get dark now and there were people walking on both sides of the road, single file. Not only this, but there were old women riding donkeys, people of all ages on bicycles and motorbikes here and there. There were no sidewalks. Some of the things that the women were carrying on their heads were large tins of water, baskets of fruit, bundles of wood and large bunches of bananas. This road fascinated me, and with all the activity on the tiny road, I found it remarkable that no one was struck by a car. This was truly a road of life. Thank God, we only encountered the "walkers" on the straight stretches, because we had enough to worry about on the crooked mountain portions. "The snake" consisted of solid rock on one side of us and a drop that was thousands of feet below on the other side, with no guard rails to prevent a car from going over the side if it veered too far. I said a prayer each time we ventured forth on that road.

Suddenly, we turned off the road, crossed a tiny bridge and pulled into a yard. We were there! This was my girlfriend's father's home. We were greeted by two dogs, two puppies, a yard boy and then the family: father, stepmother, half-brothers and sisters, nephews and nieces. It was good to be at our destination. We quickly freshened up, unpacked and dined.

That evening, accompanied by a most unforgettable native by the name of Aston Kahn, we attended an annual dance given by a sugar cane plantation, and it was quite a big affair. The band played very well and, as I glanced around me, I could not help but think that we could be at a dance in our own country; the people looked the same, the music was the same and the girls were dressed the same. Then I thought,no, there were two dead give-aways: It was very warm outside so the electric fans in the ceiling of the hall were lazily turning, and there was a Christmas tree. But even so, I felt comfortably relaxed and right at home until just before I sang.

Word had somehow gotten to Aston that I was a singer and he arranged with the bandleader for me to sing. The bandleader announced me and at the very end of his announcement he said, "And she's from America." It was at that moment that I felt the full impact or realization that I was a foreigner in a foreign land. After singing "When I Fall In Love," the audience insisted that I do another. So, being anything but shy, I then sang "Moon River," with a slow rock and roll beat. This was a first for me, the rock and roll, and it was a lot of fun. After that, I was tagged a celebrity.

The following morning we discovered the wealth surrounding our house. There were trees heavy with oranges, bananas, grapefruit, avocados, akie, tangerines, plantain, coconuts, sweet sop, sour sop and there was rice, yams, sorrel, and fields and fields of sugar cane. There were chickens, donkeys, goats, pigeons, cows, pigs and guinea pigs.

In the afternoon we drove to Montego Bay and had our first taste of the Caribbean Sea. After donning our swim suits, we went for a tour in a glass-bottom boat. The view under the water, even Walt Disney couldn't capture. Fish of all colors, sizes, shapes and forms. And the rock or coral formations were shaped like things familiar to us; for instance, a bunch of grapes, peanuts in the shell, potatoes, and there was brain coral, reindeer coral and tree coral. After this delightful tour we went swimming at Doctor's Cave, a beach in Montego Bay with its white, white sand and aqua-colored sea making quite a contrast. Only a glimpse of the poinsettia reminded me that it was Christmastime.

Late in the day we returned to Sav-La-Mar via a route other than the "snake," which took us along the coast of the Carribbean Sea. It was so picturesque, truly a living travelogue.

A few days later we made a cross-country trip in our rented Ford Zephyr to Kingston, 135 miles away. We actually crossed over a mountain. We drove like angels for fear of becoming the same. Kingston is quite a metropolis and it was interesting to see the many mixtures of people there; loads of attractive people. The motif on the Jamaican coat of arms showed very clearly here, "Out of Many, One People." The people are very warm and friendly in all of Jamaica and, although there is financial poverty among sections of the population, a high rate of unemployment and an urgent need for more development, Jamaica carries a number of assets into its newly achieved independence, as of August 6,

1962...rich soil and developing agriculture; the largest deposits of bauxite in the world; and, of course, the climate and beauty which have built the tourist trade. Christmas Eve found us back in Sav-La-Mar and on Christmas morn we attended 5 a.m. communion services at a Methodist church. The beauty of the stained glass windows at that hour left quite a lasting impression on me, not to mention the sermon. Never before had I heard that the name "Jesus" was a common name in the days when Jesus was born. I had always thought that name was exclusively His at the time of His birth and that no one was called that name before Him. We enjoyed our visit to church so much that we returned on Sunday along with the entire family, but this time it was at 11 a.m. The most outstanding part of the Sunday service was that the parson devoted about ten minutes to a story just for the children. I enjoyed it, too.

On Christmas Day, when we returned from church, two Indians arrived at the house to prepare our Christmas dinner. They caught this cute little brown and black kid, a baby goat, slit his throat, strung him up, skinned him, and made curried goat for our dinner. For those of us who had weak stomachs after watching the whole procedure, there was chicken.

The most memorable portions of our trip came whenever we were graced with the presence of Aston. He never ceased to amaze us with his thoughtfulness, generosity and wealth of information about his country and the people. He knew the right people, the right places; and if one of us mentioned that we wanted something in particular, without a word he would get it for us. Not only that, but he would also foot the bill. I am certain that each of us will never be able to think of Jamaica without thinking of Aston. I'm reminded now of an expression he always used whenever he was leaving us or saying good night, with such a nicely flavored accent, and that was "Soon Come" or "Soon Come Back." And on January 2, 1966, as I entered our plane and turned to wave good bye to our new family, I said to myself, "Soon Come."

* * *

THE ACTRESS

The two pianos complete the overture. A roll of the drums and, standing there in the wings, my knees grow weak. "My God, what am I doing here!" The curtain opens and, like magic, Eleanor becomes Babe Williams, the Grievance Committee Chairperson in Pajama Game.

Thursday, June 8, 1972; opening night, and everything going smoothly until the middle of Act I, Scene 3, where I sing "I'm Not At All In Love," my big number with all the girls. Somewhere in the middle of this number I can't think of my next line. Nothing to do but keep repeating the words that I already sung.

I feel like finding a hole and crawling into it. I can see members of the cast standing, watching in the wings. Here I am, the female lead, letting the whole cast down. What to do, what to do!

The girls in the chorus of course know I'm in trouble and finally good old Gooch comes in with the words I can't remember. The rest of the girls join in, and I pick up my lines from there to the end of the number. I actually skip the entire middle of the song.

I want to run away and hide my face forever. At the end of the scene one of the more experienced girls run to me and tells me to forget the whole "goddamn thing;" that it was over and done, and that the balance of the show was still ahead of me. I feel dizzy. I feel faint.

Somehow, I get myself together and go ahead with the show. I cannot look the cast in the eye for the rest of the first act.

At intermission, the director comes backstage. I hear him say, "Where's Eleanor?" I cover my head and face and yell, "She went home, Bill." He comes over to me, takes me by the shoulders, makes me look him in the face and says, "Tonight, you ARE a real trooper. To forget your lines like you did and yet keep right on going and then snap right back without letting it throw you, you are wonderful!" Then he kisses me right on the mouth, in front of the whole cast.

After that, I feel a hundred per cent relieved and I make it through to the finale without further disaster. The fact that everyone assures me that what happened to me happens to the best of performers really was of little help.

At the end of the show, what a surprise to learn that the audience was unaware of what actually did occur. Russ, downstage left, controlling the lighting, was unaware of the problem. At curtain call I receive two bouquets of lovely flowers; one from the court officers back at my job and one from two friends in Jersey, planning to attend the Friday performance.

Needless to say, I experience a restless sleep that night. The words that escaped me during performance went racing through my head all night, with a determination on my part not to have a repeat performance on that score.

On Friday evening, we put on a "Broadway" performance. The director almost pops all the buttons on his fancy shirt, he is so proud of us.

Saturday night audiences, as told to us by our director, are very tough. They are people who normally go to Broadway plays and they are very critical. But we sock it to the full house that night GREAT!

Sunday we do a matinee performance; a first for us. It's well attended but not as crowded as we hoped. We counted on the senior citizens who normally don't go out at night. But Sunday is a beautiful day and the benches and walkways outside are crowded with the many Jewish seniors who reside here.

The director tells us that our performances never depend on the number of people in the audience; that even if there are only two people, we have to give our best performance. So Sunday's performance is even better than the one on Saturday.

In most of Darryl's scenes, he steals the show with his antics and natural flare for the stage. And anytime we are on stage together I feel so proud. Darryl and I on stage, and Russ helping off stage!

Would you believe that two of our dear friends fly from Chicago just to see the play! Well, it's true. But in trying to surprise us, they get a surprise because they arrive a weekend too early. We feel terrible about the mistake, but spend a great weekend together and they only get to see a full rehearsal. They're unable to spend the week and wait to see the real thing. Looking back, I'm glad they were not there on opening night.

Ahead of us now, two more rehearsals and then one performance on the road this coming Saturday.

* * *

We knocked them dead, we did! Took the show on the road, all the way to Maspeth, (approximately eight miles away) and knocked them dead! That was our best performance. The Queens Arts Council donated $1000 to our group, which helped to defray some of the costs. Part of the audience came backstage afterwards and congratulated us and said that they thought they were on Broadway.

February to June-- Five months out of my life! But it was worth every moment. Believe me, it was quite an experience. And just think; I hesitated when the part was offered to me, wondering whether or not I could do it. You never know until you try.

The Rochdale Players are now trying to make me a member of the Board of Directors, but I'm afraid that's not for me. Right now, I just want to rest and then start getting acquainted with the new female in Russell's life.

Yes, Russ is in love with Celeste, his new grandchild.

Fini

Epilogue: One day, while waiting for an elevator at the courthouse where I work, a young white girl approached me and said, "Are you an actress?" I smiled, thinking she had mistaken me for someone else. I said, "Where?" She replied, "Off Broadway." "Yeah," I said, "way, way off Broadway." She then remarked, "I saw you in a play at Maspeth High School about a year ago."

SUMMER VACATION 1973

A fresh rose lay on the white linen cloth that covered the eating tray. The volume on my ear phones was so loud that any minute I expected someone to tap me on the shoulder and complain. When no one showed any sign of disturbance, I leaned back in my seat, stared out into the blue, blue sky and marvelled at the scattered white puffy clouds. Then I closed my eyes and there I was smack in the middle of a full orchestra playing beautiful classical music.

That's how our vacation began-- United Airlines, first class! After dining on gourmet food and enjoying the service and the music, five hours later we landed in Seattle. Or I should say the plane and everyone in it landed, except Russell. What with scotch on the rocks, scotch and soda, scotch and water, white wine, red wine, and champagne, Russell was still flying when we landed. He just kept saying, "Beautiful flight! Beautiful flight!" And even with his new teeth, that wasn't too clear.

Five days in Seattle with grandma, and we had had it. On to San Francisco. A ride on the ferry to Sausalito where I had my fill of German chocolate cake ice cream, apple strudle ice cream, and strawberry cheesecake ice cream; and where Russ almost got "picked up" by a Japanese fellow. A visit to the new Regency Hyatt House Hotel with its most unusual lobby and outside elevators made of glass. Shopping at I. Magnin's.

Then one morning at 10:30 a friend of Uncle Ronnie's picked us up at our Holiday Inn located right in the heart of China Town and off we went on a private guided tour; from San Francisco Bay to the Pacific Ocean (first time I was ever that close to the Pacific). Telegraph Hill. Lombard Street, the most crooked street in the world. Fisherman's Warf. Chiaradelli Square. The Wax Museum. Seal Rock.

Our private tour ended at the Top of the Mark (if not the swankiest hotel in Frisco, a close second) where we were treated to cocktails and then back down to the lobby where we were treated to lunch; my own consisting of the most delicious hot fudge sundae! We were then returned to our hotel at 3:30 p.m. with the apologies of our congenial host that he had to be at work at 4 p.m. and who repeated how sorry his wife was that she was unable to join us.

At 8:30 the same evening, too tired to go out and since we had to be up early the next morning, we were lounging when the ringing of the telephone startled us. Russ looked at me and I looked at him. It turned out to be the wife of the gentleman who showed us the town; and she and I gabbed just as if we had known each other all our lives.

Four days later found us at the bus terminal in San Francisco, en route to the airport, when I heard someone say "Why, Mrs. Speer!" Seven o'clock in the morning! Who on earth-- Imagine my surprise when I turned around and saw a young man from New York that I had taught in Sunday School years ago!

One-half hour later we breakfasted at the airport and Russ had an interesting conversation with an Eskimo who lived in Alaska. An hour's ride, and we were in Las Vegas with its 102-degree temperature. There we met two other couples, one by pre-arrangement; from Chicago. To our surprise, my aunt and uncle from Chicago had come along also. It was so good to see them! Together we saw the Liza Minelli Show, the Elvis Pressley Show, the Kim sisters and the Wilson Pickett Show. And I had a hundred-dollar win at Keno. Three days later we were winging our way back to New York.

Four days at home and off again, this time to Sewickley, Pa.; outside of Pittsburgh. Immediately upon arrival we were driven to a studio where we enjoyed a live jazz set, a command performance just for us, which lasted two hours. A piano, a regular bass, an electric guitar, drums and a trumpet. Five music teachers preparing their modus operandi for the coming term were nice enough to do a "first" for us. The fellow on the guitar sounded just like Wes Montgomery. And later that evening we discovered that his guitar had indeed been given to him by Wes himself. Our second day brought a visit to a speed boat owned by our host and hostess. It's a little sports cruiser, sleeps two; and is the fastest boat on the river there in Pittsburgh.

Ever drifted along on a small boat on a hot summer's night with beautiful music flowing from a tape, and the city lights sparkling like precious stones in the reflection of the water? It was the most peaceful and relaxed moments of our vacation; just what the doctor ordered, if you know what I mean.

They lived on a hilltop, about twenty minutes from town; a beautiful ranch, two-level, eleven-room home. And our third day found me driving their small tractor to mow the grass on their acre of land. Everything was so informal and comfortable that it was like home away from home.

I always had a secret desire to drive a huge Mack truck, and our fourth day found me behind the wheel of just that, a huge Mack truck. Only had my picture taken in it though; too many gears to try and drive it. It was owned by our host.

That evening we played bid whist, after another spin on the boat. We played from 1 a.m. to 7 a.m. Russ had bragged that he and I were the best in the east and the people we were playing with swore that they were the best in the west; so we played for six hours and ended in a tie. Our last day was spent shooting pool on Henry's brand new pool table, weeding the back yard, shopping, and chasing their Dachshund around the house. We made sandwiches for dinner. And at 7:15, p.m. we were sadly on our way to the airport to return home. It was the greatest summer we've ever had.

* * *

HOME FOR MOTHER'S DAY

One hour out of Kennedy Airport and my plane is landing in Norfolk, Virginia. The papers are pulled for my reserved Hertz car; directions gotten, and before you can say gesundheit, here I am driving down Military Highway in a cute little orange-yellow Maverick heading for Route 17 which will carry me 90 miles south, right to my home town in North Carolina.

This car isn't bad at all, but I sure wish I had the power brakes on my beautiful new dark-brown and tan Thunderbird back in New York.

Friday morning and 65 degrees; a beautiful day. This is great. The roads in New York should be so empty. Follow the signs now; you're both pilot and navigator. Pick out some landmarks for the return drive. Make it easy on yourself.

"Vicky's Palace." Good. Wonder how our Vicky's doing. Wouldn't mind seeing them, especially the baby. No trouble remembering that landmark anyway.

Hey! Route 17. A complete stop now. Take a look. Wow! Here comes a moving van and is he moving. I'll get behind him and hang onto his tail. Two-lane blacktop; speed, 55. Hope there are no slow pokes. "Speed checked by radar." Keep your eyes peeled, girl; remember the police testimony about radar in traffic court. The little box, the parked car with the open trunk.

Better turn on the radio. Close the windows, put the air conditioning on low.

Loads of trees on either side, beautiful blue sky, and the open road. Say, it's just like the picture postcard that Uncle Ronnie sent me last time he was down here. What a good feeling, what freedom! Am I glad I listened to Russ; "Better rent a car and then you'll have it to get around in when you get there."

Let's see; left Norfolk at 10:25. Should be in Plymouth by 12:25 p.m. Bet my mother's on pins and needles. Haven't seen her since Christmas 1972. Or was it 1971? Hope she likes her Mother's Day present.

Remember to call Mr. Freeman's office tomorrow, see if any progress can be made on the mobile home. God, how they need a place to live. A two-bedroom will be great. Room for Russ and I when we visit, too. If only I can find a vacant lot in town within walking distance of Aunt Helen!

Heck, there goes the moving van. How dare he turn off when I'm only half-way home! Say, got the whole road to myself. Imagine! Wouldn't like to be caught out here at night though.

Sure hope I'm in good voice for this Mother's Day present. Me and my bright ideas! Wonder who's playing for me.

"Plymouth 20 miles." I can do that with my eyes closed.

Say, I'm home. Slow down, get your bearings. Now Cousin Clara lives there, so this would be where the old train station used to be; where I used to meet the train and sell the passengers our huge delicious plums-- a whole coffee-can full for a quarter. The same train my doll and I would take to Elizabeth City, some 30 miles away, to spend two weeks with Aunt Ida during the summer; traveling in care of the conductor. You've come a long way, baby!

Make a right at the light. What's this; a traffic jam in little old Plymouth? Oh, the freight train! Got here in two hours, only to be held up by a freight train. Remember when you used to get such a thrill counting the cars on the freight train? That was a long time ago.

Nothing to do but wait. Look around you. Quite a shopping center out here now. Everything's so different. There goes the caboose, finally. Cross the tracks, go one block; turn right, two blocks down, make another right; cross back over the tracks, and there's my mother at the door.

Say, she's not as grey as I thought she'd be. And she's about the same size as when I last saw her; five feet tall and wearing a size 18½ dress. She looks well, thank God. Relief in her face that I arrived safely. Hugs, kisses, home!

Unpack, eat lunch (chicken and potato salad); then off to see Aunt Helen, Uncle Zion and Aunt Minerva. Back to the house. Freshen up. Take a nap. Well, relax anyway-- run through the papers and see if there are any houses for sale.

So BurlyBee Moore is going to play for me, according to Aunt Helen. Gee, we went to grammar school together. Too bad we can't go over this music till Sunday. And I came right through Elizabeth City where he lives. Now stop! Whatcha getting nervous so soon for!

New Chapel Baptist Church. Mother's Day, 1974. Church is crowded, jammed pack. My goodness, what am I in for? Mother looks at me and asks if I'm nervous and I say, "Of course." Then I look at her and she seems more nervous than I.

The bulletin simply says "Solo." I'm on. Unannounced. The introduction on the organ. Then I sing "If I Can Help Somebody." I can't see my mother from the choir box where I'm standing, but I can see people's heads leaning and necks stretching as if to say "Wonder who that is singing." All eyes on me. Must have been at least 225 to 250 people there to hear my mother's Mother's Day gift.

* * *

SUMMER 1974

After cancelling our trip to Barbados and substituting Atlanta and Tallahassee, we ended up in Barbados after all; a glorious paradise island full of lush, shiny greenery and all kinds of strange colorful flowers and trees and delicious fruits: Palm trees and coconut trees, mango and bananas trees, paw paw and breadfruit; trees called Pride-of-Barbados with their bursts of bright yellow flowers; and Pride-of-India trees with their bursts of red flowers.

Where warm sea breezes always blow from the Atlantic to the Caribbean and vice versa.

Where the rain showers are so short that if you're dancing on an open-air dance floor, you just step to the side under shelter and wait a few minutes until the rain stops and then you continue dancing, puddles and all. The band never stops playing.

Where you don't say you're going to the beach, but "to the sea" or you take a "sea bath."

Where the sea water is green and so clean and clear that you can see the bottom; and where the natives drink a wee bit of the salty sea water for whatever ails them. Where all the beaches are open to the public, poor and rich alike, and they're free.

Where the natives speak with a sing-song soft, smooth lilt that falls on the ear like music.

Where the females put deep, deep hems in their dresses to make them ever so short because the weather is so hot.

Where many old women carry large bundles of fruits and vegetables or just about anything on their heads, with not even one hand holding it. I saw one woman with a 30-pound bag of flour.

Where the streets are so narrow that two compact cars can barely make it passing in opposite directions and yet people on bicycles and on foot crowd into the little streets. You wonder why the pedestrians don't move out of the way of moving traffic, until you realize there's no place for them to move. There are no sidewalks except in the downtown shopping area.

Where you pay $2 a year for a license to ride a bicycle. Where our dollar is worth almost two of theirs.

Where wages are so low and prices so high that you wonder how the people manage. For instance, a large can of Planter's peanuts cost $3.60 in their money (equal to about $1.80 in our money) as compared to 79 cents that we pay in the States for the same size can.

Where the buses have open-air windows on both sides (no glass), which is just great because hardly any natives use deoderant. They obviously can't afford to buy deoderant or soap on thc money they make.

Where some of the young native men don't have jobs, but make their living by escorting female tourists "wherever" they wish to go. The tourists pay his way. The Canadian female tourists seem to have a monopoly on this practice.

Where the whole country is filled with little huts of one room, just large enough to hold a small bed and a chest and maybe a chair. They're known as eight by tens, or something similar; probably eight feet by ten feet.

Where nobody rushes, but nobody; especially the waiters.

Where the absence of the white man boss is conspicuous, and nice, for a change.

* * *

HIS WIFE, THE BRIDGE PLAYER

There were people from California, Illinois, Georgia, Michigan, Washington, D.C., Louisiana, Nevada, Virginia, New York, New Jersey, Missouri, Maryland, Texas, Kentucky, Ohio, Barbados, Hawaii; you name it, they were there.

The atmosphere at the Waldorf Astoria Hotel was warm and friendly and filled with great expectation. Friends who hadn't seen each other since the last National Bridge Tournament were hugging and kissing and telling each other lies-- all very exciting.

It was Friday, August 8, 1975, the first day of a week long tournament of the American Bridge Association, and a first ever for me.

So this is what I gave up a week of my summer vacation for, and any plans to leave the city. This was it?!

For one week I played duplicate bridge with new players like myself (kibitizers) from 1 p.m. to 5 p.m.; stopped for dinner and played again from 8 p.m. to midnight. And then there were parties almost every night after the games. I couldn't make all the parties because I then had to drive back to Queens to try to get some sleep so I could play the following day. By Thursday, I had had it, so I moved into the hotel for the final weekend of the tournament.

Each evening when I returned home (or I should say each morning) Russ would give me a big kiss and then grin and say, "My wife, the bridge player!" And in the next breath, "Did you win?"

Poor guy; he was on his own all week. I would put food on to cook in the crock pot while I slept so he didn't have to eat out. And on a couple of occasions he met me at the hotel around dinner time and we would have dinner together. He would then stay in the city with friends and meet me around midnight and we would go home together.

He really couldn't complain because he pushed me into bridge. Actually, the both of us started classes together way back in 1969 and he dropped out saying it was "too many damn things to remember." I kept going for a short while and then I dropped out because I never knew who my partner was going to be or even if I would have a partner when I got to class.

In 1973 one of our neighbors asked me to attend bridge classes with her, so I started again. This lasted a few months and then the neighbor dropped out. So again I dropped out.

In 1974 Russ kept asking me (almost every Tuesday evening) "Why don't you go down to the club and play bridge tonight?" And I would get annoyed with him trying to push me when he had given up entirely. At least I would read the bridge column in the newspaper every day. Then in 1975 he would tell me that certain people would be my partner if I went down to play, because he had already set it up.

Later, in 1975, when I heard that the National Tournament was to be held in New York City in August I became genuinely interested again. I took myself to another bridge class in June, 1975, each Wednesday night. Gradually, things began to fall into place and I was actually beginning to feel I finally had the hang of it. So I read and I practiced by myself; I bugged a guy at work who is a top player; I lived bridge, thought bridge, talked bridge, dreamt bridge from June to August with the idea of playing at the Nationals.

Well, it paid off, because at the Nationals my partner, Delores, and I won two trophies and about seven points. But "it wasn't easy, ma." The tournament was comparable to a crash course in bridge. I made a lot of mistakes, learned a heck of a lot about the game, about people, about myself; met a whole bunch of nice people from all over the country, and had the time of my life!

The whole idea of playing bridge began with the thought that if I learn now, when I retire from work and after I can no longer sing, I'll at least be a GOOD bridge player. And as you can see, I'm hooked!

At the Awards Ball, which closes the tournament, while dancing with Russ, he said, "Baby, maybe this winter you can teach me how to play bridge."

* * *

THE OTHER SIDE

by: Eleanor Speer

What's taking those two men at the check-in counter so long? No wonder the airline wanted us to check in two hours ahead of time! A woman is beckoned over. It seems that she has packed their passports in one of the suitcases. Which one? She takes out the key to the suitcase; is sure of where she put the passports, but they're not there. They open a second suitcase and rummage through that. They find the passports.

Meanwhile a tall, shapely, beautiful gal hurries over; looks around and discovers that one of her bags is situated in the middle of our bags. She checks the name on the tag; looks up at us, smiles. and says, "He's leaving my bag behind!"

Five minutes later, a gong goes off in my head. I say to Russ; "See if the first name on that tag is Laverne," referring to the bag which the gal had just pushed away from us. He checks; and it is.

After seeing that the two men were just about finished checking in and that the beautiful gal had joined one of the men, I say in an irritated fashion, "Laverne, what's taking you so long? She turns, and in a split second she says, "Eleanor!"

Smiles, introductions, et cetera, et cetera. We were going to be on the same flight. Laverne Holt and Eleanor Exum, our maiden names. Mother Zion Junior Church Choir in Harlem, soprano section. Thirty years since we've seen each other!

After stopping in Baltimore to pick up additional passengers we (Ed & Eltrude; Freddie & Evelyn; Ted & Joyce; Rick & Vivian; Penny, Pam, Lillian, Joan & George; Chuck & Jackie, Russ & Ellie, Tony & Bernice; and Bob & Erma) continued on our fly/cruise to San Juan, Puerto Rico; the first leg of a cruise the whole bunch of us planned way back in November, 1975. In Puerto Rico, we were met by buses that carried us to our ships. It was on the plane that I learned that Laverne would be sailing on the Amerikanis and we would be on the Carla "C;" but that our ships would be docking in three of the same ports at the same time. Also, we would be returning to New York on the same air flight.

We sailed at midnight Saturday, July 10th, and were at sea all day and all night Sunday. Sunday morning I went to the chapel aboard ship at 11:10 and waited for the all-denominational service to begin. Service was scheduled for 11:15. At 11:20 the clergyman turned, looked at me, smiled, and in a very thick foreign accent said, "Nobody come!" I looked him straight in the eye and replied, "We're here;" meaning just he and I. So he stood up, faced me, and started reading from a devotional-type book. By the time he completed his first reading the little chapel was practically filled. There were nice new hymnals on every other seat and he asked us to open to #1 and sing Holy, Holy, Holy. After he read the scripture he looked over his glasses and beckoned in my direction. I turned my head to see if he meant someone in back of me because people were now standing in the rear of the chapel. I then pointed to myself as if to say "Who, me?" and he nodded his head yes.

I walked up front, accepted the book he offered me and began to read the indicated passage. After thinking for a fleeting moment of how ridiculous I must look standing there in shorts and sunglasses, I became quite composed. In fact, I began to enjoy it when I noticed that the audience seemed really to be listening to every word.

Monday morning we docked in Curacao. After breakfast Russ and I were met at the ship by two beautiful people who are natives of Curacao; Pansy and Carl, friends of my Uncle Ronnie. They took a day off from their jobs, just for us, and gave us a grand tour of Curacao in their comfortable, air-conditioned, American car.

Curacao is a very pretty island, clean and neat. It is divided by a river, and one side is called "The Other Side." They have a floating pontoon bridge, a foot bridge (no cars allowed) that slowly swings out from one side into the water towards "The Other Side" when ships have to go through. It's fascinating to watch, and I imagine even more fascinating to be caught on the bridge when it swings to "The Other Side."

Curacao also has a most unique and modern three tier, open air market where all kinds of fresh foods are sold, and it's the cleanest market I've ever seen.

Water is very precious there and very expensive; mainly because of the desalienation process that their water must go through and the low rate of waterfall. Many people have cisterns built in their backyards to catch rainwater, which they use for washing clothes or watering their lawns, et cetera.

After treating us to a huge, delicious lunch at a Chinese restaurant, Carl and Pansy took us to their home, a lovely, spacious, modern home, furnished in excellent taste, surrounded by lush greenery; among which was an almond tree. I had never seen an almond tree and was quite surprised at its beauty and how much the leaves resemble leaves of the Magnolia tree. I sampled fruit of another tree, the texture of which was like a combination of a peach and an apple, and which tasted like ice cream. And to my detriment, I promtly began to break out in hives.

Practically everything in Curacao has to be imported. And I learned that most of Carl and Pansy's furnishings came from Sears Roebuck of Philadelphia.

Although the weather was terribly hot, a delightful cool breeze blew right through their home. And while we sat talking, getting to know one another it was all I could do to try and stay awake. Late in the afternoon they returned us to our ship, where they joined us in a farewell drink before we sailed at 7 p.m.

Tuesday we docked in Caracas, Venezuela. Here we took an all-day tour, which included, among other things, a cable car ride which carried us 14,000 feet above sea level to the top of the Andes Mountains. When we reached the top, we looked down into the clouds and the sky on one side and on "The Other Side" we looked down into the beautiful modern city of Caracas. And even with the wind whipping all around us, there was an overwhelming sense of serenity and peacefulness at the very top.

But all was not peaceful when our cable car came down from the mountain. A senior citizen who sat directly in front of us on our tour bus, but who chose not to go up on the cable car, had been accidentally knocked down and run over by one of the tour buses. All sorts of stories reached us. We heard that she was 81 years old; that the bus had mangled her leg; that no one seemed excited when it happened; that a taxi driver had grabbed her purse and ran to his cab with it and then came back and returned an empty purse; that the police had finally arrived and ordered an ambulance and that the lady had been taken to a hospital.

Needless to say, we were all shaken, especially the tour guide. The sad part though was that the victim was traveling alone; she was on our ship but none of us knew her name or where she was from, or what language she spoke--just nothing at all. We learned the following day that she died. And the day we left Puerto Rico, on our return home, the person in charge of our flight announced that everyone was accounted for except one person and that we would wait another fifteen minutes for that person. Then we all realized we were waiting for a woman who would never show.

After the tragedy in Caracas, we were taken to lunch at one of the large American hotels, where we were joined by many, many bus loads of tourists from several ships. The food was good and we had musical entertainment while we dined. Just before the music started an announcement was made in English, Spanish and French that some traveler's checks had been found and whether anyone in this huge dining hall had lost the same. Freddie, a loud, loquacious, jolly fellow in our group said, "What idiot would lose his traveler's checks." Much to his chagrin, he turned out to be the idiot, and was oh so embarrassed when he had to walk up to the microphone in front of the entire audience to claim his checks.

We docked in Trinidad on Wednesday. Our plan was to visit a friend, but when we called his home his wife informed us that he had expected us on the 24th, not the 14th; that he was now in Jamaica, W.I. and was returning home that evening. They lived too far in the country for us to try to get there on our own, so that was that, especially since we were sailing at 5 p.m.

Anyway, Russ went off with the boys and I went shopping with the girls. And that was my mistake. We took a taxi, the driver of which got downright belligerent when we refused his services to "show" us Trinidad. We couldn't wait to get to the main shopping area so we could be rid of him. And when we got there, the sidewalks were so crowded with poor people selling their wares and staring at us as if to say "Those ugly Americans," and the heat was so intense; all this, coupled with my dislike for shopping in the first place, sent me scurrying back to the air-conditioned ship in no time at all.

When our fellows returned from their private tour by cab, they told us of the posh sections they had seen and how they sat in the bar at the golf course and were not allowed to talk because the sound of their voices might drift onto the "greens," where a tournament was being held, and that that might distract the players; how someone unintentionally scraped their chair along the floor and everybody turned around and went "Shhhhhhhh!" All very, very British.

On Thursday we dropped anchor in Martinique, where it's necessary to take a tender to go ashore because large ships cannot go all the way to the dock.

On the day we sailed from Puerto Rico, I knew for a fact that my Aunt Lil from Chicago and her hubby would also be sailing from Miami on the Nordic Prince; in celebration of her retirement from the teaching profession. I did not have their itinerary but planned to look for their ship every place we docked. I knew theirs was a two-week cruise whereas ours was one week.

In Martinique I decided I'd stay aboardship, sleep late, relax, have the pool to myself, write a couple of cards, read a little, the whole bit. At about 11 a.m. I came alive, went topside and watched the passengers load into tenders to go ashore. It was a gorgeous day, a beautiful port. No other ships were in sight; only small, private pleasure craft. I lazed around, enjoying every moment. Russ went ashore, but returned in two hours. We had lunch and I lounged some more. Then he reminded me that the program for the day mentioned that native dancers were coming aboardship at 3:30 to do a show for us and that everyone was planning to watch them. Those who went ashore had to be back early anyway because we were sailing at 6 p.m.

The dancers came and did beautiful folklore dances for us, using their native French, which was explained to us in three different languages before each dance began.

When the show ended close to 5 p.m. and the audience didn't want the dancers to leave, our cruise director made this announcement: "Thank them again, gang, but let them go because the passengers on the NORDIC PRINCE, on "The Other Side" of town, are waiting for them to do a show before they sail at 7 p.m."

I turned to Russ. We stared at each other. First, I accused him of not seeing Sis (that's what I call my aunt) shopping somewhere when he went ashore; or didn't he bump into anyone from the Nordic Prince, etc., etc., etc. I was only teasing him.

Next, I ran to the radio room, caught the guy in charge in a bathing suit leaving with some chick; interrupted them long enough to ask could I make a telephone call to the Nordic Prince. He apologized, saying everything is always closed down whenever the ships are in harbor. So I wanted to know what about when we started to sail; could I do it then. And he said maybe, but that the Nordic Prince would be sailing one hour after us, plus they were going in the opposite direction.

Well, what now? No time to take a tender to shore and no guarantee they would be aboardship. So I quick, wrote a postcard, one of those free ones with a picture of our ship on it, the Carla "C;" addressed it to "Mrs. Lillian Bray, Nordic Prince: (put that day's date on the card) Hi! Love, Ellieboo." (Ooops, revealing more family secrets.) I then ran down to the Main Deck where the dancers were going down the gangplank to enter the tenders. I took a dollar from my purse, approached one of the pretty young things and said, "Parle vous Anglais?" She stared at me and said, "No." Then I thought to myself, one of them has to speak English--maybe the man who seemed to be in charge of them. So I waited for him to head for the tender. There he is. "Monsieur, parle-vous Anglais?" He smiled and said yes. So I pushed the card and the dollar into his hand, begging him to please give the card to anyone on the Nordic Prince when they arrived for the show, and he promised he would.

I don't know how I went to sleep that night. I hadn't seen my aunt for a couple of years. And the one day I decide to stay aboardship, we're in the same port at the same time. I can't see her ship from my ship because we're on opposite sides of the harbor. She's going one way, and I'm going the other. Incidentally, she vaguely knew we were on a cruise, but did not know the time or the name of the ship.

Friday we docked in St. Thomas, Virgin Islands. Right away, I felt we were in the States. After doing our "big" shopping (liquor and a gold chain and earrings), we called St. Croix to say hello to a friend from New York who was vacationing there the entire summer. A half hour later Russ and I were picked up by an ex-neighbor of mine who is now retired and lives in St. Thomas. We spent a lovely day with them; Vera and I chatting about the old neighborhood, while her husband Clarence and Russ got to know one another.

Vera is crippled from arthritis, but she's one of the finest hostesses I know. At different intervals while we sat talking she would disappear into the kitchen and in a few moments come back with one of her gourmet gems. First came frozen pineapple wedges, frozen in gin. Russ loved them. Next came fresh toasted coconut. It was delicious. Then came homemade herb cheese balls stuck with toothpicks and toasted almonds from their own tree.

Around five o'clock she set an attractive table and we sat down to a light dinner of chicken salad filled with water chestnuts and pineapple pieces; heart of palm, tomato wedges, sliced boiled eggs, dilled asparagus spears, hot rolls, ice tea, and homemade apricot brandy chiffon pie. She said she wanted to have something different from what we were having on the ship, and she succeeded beautifully. In fact, she outdid herself.

At midnight we sailed for Puerto Rico; went through customs by 10:30 a.m. Saturday morning; checked in at the airport and had a four-hour wait before flight time. One of the couples that we met aboardship, and who turned out to be neighbors back in Jamaica where we live, knew we would have the wait-over, so they invited all 21 of us to come to their condominium in Puerto Rico, where they were going to spend the next two weeks, and which was only five minutes riding time from the airport.

Some of us felt a bit awkward about all of us piling into one apartment and Russ and I were reluctant to go; that is, until we realized that everyone else had disappeared in little groups. Besides, I knew Russ was anxious to see what the place looked like; so off we went.

It was located next to the El San Juan Hotel, and the place was simply fantabulous. With the 21 of us there, plus four others who were sharing the apartment for two weeks, there was still room for about 20 more without the place being crowded. And from the terrace, which was almost as large as the living room, we looked right down into the blue-green sea and white sand and there was practically nobody on the beach. It was breathtakingly beautiful, to say the least. Everyone vowed that this was the place for our next vacation--rent a condo for a week.

At one hour prior to check-in time at the airport our group piled into several taxis and headed for the airport.

Except for having to wait two extra hours before take-off, and aside from one of our stewardesses getting seriously ill aboard plane and an ambulance waiting in Baltimore to pick her up; and aside from our plane conking out in Baltimore and our having to transfer to another airline; the return flight was uneventful.

* * *

EPILOGUE:

One Tuesday evening early in August I received a phone call. It was from my Aunt Lil in Chicago. This is what she said: "Ellieboo, how on earth did you ever get that card to us on our ship?"

She told how she and her hubby were in their cabin dressing for dinner when the card came sliding under their door; how her hubby said, "Baby, we have some mail;" how she said "Mail? What do you mean, mail?" how they picked up the card, read it, turned it over, saw Carla "C," turned it back over, saw that day's date, no postmark; and how utterly flabbergasted they were; how she upset practically the entire ship, demanding an explanation as to how the card had reached her....and....whether she could get a card to me on my ship the same way.

* * *

CHRISTMAS

He's in his mid-forties. A circular bed in various VA hospitals has been his home for nearly fifteen years. Crippling rheumatoid arthritis of the spine. He's totally paralyzed, but he can talk and sing and laugh and cry.

All the little things we take for granted: to feed ourselves, to light a cigarette, to scratch an itch, to turn on the radio or television, to even pick up a telephone-- denied him forever.

His wife, unable to cope, walked away years ago, shortly after the birth of a daughter. That thirteen-year-old visits once a year. Her mother has remarried.

The pain is all gone now. Maybe it's because his once normal, full sized body has atrophied to that of a nine-year-old. But the years of suffering have not destroyed his brilliant, clear mind.

It's a few days before Christmas. The dinner dishes are being washed. The phone rings. The operator asks for me. I acknowledge. The operator says, "The line is open, sir." And the next sound I hear is that strong, hearty, rich voice of my friend, Peter Watt.

* * *

PONDERING

About sex yes Peter does think about sex now as well as during the days when he was married to Ann and when their daughter was born and when he became totally paralyzed and when one year two years went by and when Ann divorced him and when four years five years went by and Ann remarried and when ten years went by and Ann died and now when after twenty years on his back unable to move naught but the index finger on one hand oh the irony now of his penis erecting, so he says.

* * *

A Weekend With Amy

At 2:30 in the afternoon our plane landed. It looked like the middle of nowhere. The hot sun felt good as we walked to the terminal. Russ heeded a call of nature en route to the luggage pick-up area, which made us the last passengers to enter the actual terminal.

We approached Amy who was waiting for us at the entrance to the boarding area. She wore an expression of bewilderment and disappointment. She had not seen us as yet and it was obvious that she thought we had missed the plane. We delighted at the prospect of being able to surprise her by suddenly appearing just when she decided that we had not arrived. She looked first one way and then the other. Her eyes were searching the crowd waiting for their luggage and then gazing off in the direction from whence they had come.

When she finally spotted us, she uttered a visible sigh of relief and placed her hands on her hips, pursed her lips, and pulled her body up even straighter than usual. With her right hand, she pointed a finger at us, as if to scold us for giving her those few anxious moments when she thought we had missed the plane, or whatever.

We reached each other and there were greetings and hugs and the three of us bubbled over with happiness, all speaking at the same time. "So this is Tallahassee! Where's the town?" I said. And Russ added, "Where's the airport?" And Amy playfully hit him on top of his head.

We left the airport and proceeded by car. In about twenty minutes we pulled off the quiet country road into a circular driveway which, at its halfway point, became a carpet attached to a beautiful sprawling ranch house tucked among tall, slender pine trees.

Entering through the front door into a spacious hallway area with wood-paneled walls covered with unique hand carvings and paintings, immediately to the left was the master bedroom with its private bath. Straight ahead was the "open" kitchen with a snack bar. Then came the living room with a music closet. Off the living room was an alcove type area with a full bath, a library, and a small bedroom/office. Walking to the right we entered an eating area off the kitchen which combined with the music room. Amy's black Baby Grand piano stood in a room with a cornflower blue velvet couch, on an olive green wall-to-wall rug. The room had three white walls and a fourth wall of glass which extended from floor to ceiling and which faced out upon a patio and a view of nature's splendor in May.

The clear, blue sky was visible through the top of the pines. And at their feet lay a huge back yard with flower gardens. As we strolled outside, we found a vegetable garden. In addition, there were all kinds of plants and shrubs surrounding the entire house.

In mid-April Amy had called to ask if we could come visit her the weekend of May 12th, 1978; that we just had to come! We thought there was to be a wedding. But no; it was just that if we could come that weekend she would know what to do with us as opposed to any other weekend. She had told us that there was to be a big party Saturday evening; that 26 couples were coming from Atlanta for a club meeting/party, and Amy was invited and could bring us along. We could come visit her on any day and stay as long as we wanted, as long as we were there on that particular Saturday.

It was soon 4 p.m. and Amy proceeded to give us a run-down of what she had in store for us. At 5 p.m. we were to be officially introduced to Tallahassee at a cocktail party in our honor. Twenty odd persons had been invited to her home and we had to "dress" for the occasion. At 7 p.m. the guests would leave and we would change clothes. Later we were to have dinner at a restaurant with one other person, and after dinner we would be joined by another couple and in a different part of the restaurant we would see a show and dance the night away.

Saturday morning we were to breakfast out, and at 10 a.m. we would take a tour of Florida's capital. Later we would do a little grocery shopping because two people were coming for cocktails at 5 p.m. and yet another couple would arrive for dinner at 6 p.m. By ten we would be on our way to the party that the entire trip had been planned around.

Sunday, at noon, the couple instrumental in Amy's appointment as a Professor of Music at Florida State University would come for brunch, and we would eventually leave on the 3:30 flight that afternoon.

Friday's cocktail party was a classy affair. We met instructors and their spouses, students, housewives, a policeman who was an ex-New Yorker, and loads of musicians. Perhaps the splendid array of musical talent inhibited each musician, or possibly everyone was having such a wonderful time that no one approached the piano to play for us. Amy served several homemade quiche Lorraines and champagne filled with whole fresh strawberries.

Following the cocktail party, Amy took us to a fairly new restaurant that specialized in fine seafood. The oysters were scrumptious. And I put a hurting on the salad bar, the bread bar and the sherbet bar. Amy was a delight and gracious hostess, and as we sat luxuriating in the warm, friendly atmosphere of the evening, Russ and I could not help commenting to each other about the changes that had taken place in the deep south; black and white sitting at the same tables, even dancing with one another, in a first-rate establishment that catered to people rather than to race.

Everything went according to schedule on Friday, but as we dragged ourselves to bed at 5 a.m. Saturday morning, Russ and I realized that we could never be up early, and we told Amy that we would fix our own breakfast when we did arise. We awoke at noon, and I fixed breakfast. Other than this one deviation, we followed Amy's plans in every respect.

The big bash Amy took us to was held at a spacious home in a new, well-to-do area of Tallahassee. I had been told in advance about "the bus" in which the club members had arrived, but I didn't really believe it until our car turned onto the street where the party was to be held. Sure enough, right in front of the house there sat a big beautiful bus with Georgia license plates. It looked so out of place that the picture of it will linger in my mind for a long time. The neighbors had no grounds for complaint though, because all was quiet from the outside. But when the door of the house was opened to us, the place was jumping. The club meeting had concluded and everyone was partying. A few people had spilled out onto the back patio for a bit of fresh air, but those inside were having a ball. Again we danced all night-- even Russ. He was really on cloud nine because a beautiful lady tried to "pick him up." It was a great party, but of course the evening had to come to an end.

The next morning we arose about ten o'clock to find Amy deep into several cookbooks. Russ and I packed, and after the arrival of two close friends of Amy's, we had a very delicious brunch of eggs Tarragon served on toasted English muffins with Canadian bacon on the side.

All too soon it was time for Amy to drive us to the airport, and once there, we bid a bittersweet farewell to each other and the 3:30 flight whisked us back to our workaday lives.

* * *

Epilogue: At the airport, while waiting to board our plane, Amy suddenly started to cry uncontrollably. She couldn't explain why. It was all very disconcerting. She never saw Russell again except to attend his funeral in New York on October 16, 1978.

THE CHRISTMAS *THAT WAS*

(A Dream Come True)

There he was, seated at the head of the table; tall, dark and handsome, with his silver hair and his infectious smile. On his right sat wife #1; on his left, wife #3; and, serving the Christmas dinner, was wife #2. Twentytwo people in all--family, childhood friends with their children, neighbors--and he was in his glory. My father.

Talk about timing! Fifteen years ago this would not have been possible. But isn't it wonderful how time heals so many wounds.

As long as I live, there will never be another day like Christmas 1979--A dream come true.

My mother Nettie (wife #1) had come from North Carolina to spend Christmas with me. Bea (wife #2) came to dinner and brought her boyfriend. And daddy came and brought Dottie (wife #3).

Never was there a more festive, magical day; a once-in-a-lifetime happening, where all the ingredients blended so perfectly that one couldn't help but marvel and enjoy.

* * *

TRIBUTE

Sunday, January 31, 1982

Good timing; 2:50 p.m. Ten minutes before curtain time and all these empty seats? Benefit crowd. Late crowd. Not your usual Carnegie Hall patron.

Where are my opera glasses? Let's see if Marian is here. Ah! There she is, in the box just above right-stage. My, but she looks terrific. The audience hasn't discovered her yet. Wait. Yes; they see her now. The audience is applauding.

Curtain time. Say, the hall is full! Only two empty boxes remain. Here comes the female conductor. Applause. She's kinda cute. Out comes Grace Bumbry in a Chinese red gown, followed by Shirley Verrett in black chiffon. Thunderous applause! Tremendous applause! Not a chord has been struck, and all this applause! They're beautiful. The artists and the audience. A duet; then Grace, then Shirley, then the orchestra; another duet. Beautiful. They're trying to out-sing each other. Intermission.

Cameras popping, newsmen everywhere, TV cameras all over the place. Even John Q. Public crowding around; all vying for a photo of Marian. Total quietness. Comments by Isaac Stern, President of Carnegie Hall, for this special tribute. Two Written messages read by Mr. Stern; one from Mayor Koch, and one from President Reagan. A sudden loud, male voice from the first balcony singing Happy Birthday To You. The whole audience joins in. All except me. I'm fighting back tears of emotion. Come on girl, get yourself together. Blow your nose. Blow hard.

The conductor is back. She's good. Grace enters in a different red gown, with mink cuffs; and Shirley in white, with feathers off each shoulder. Didn't really expect a fashion show, too. Outrageous applause! A little embarrassing.

On with the show. A glorious afternoon. The battle of two so-called rival black opera stars. Unbelievable applause, as the stars embrace. Never appeared on stage together before today. The audience eats it up, and brings them back for an encore. Finis. The end of a magical afternoon.

If only my talent and love for music had been discovered or recognized in my childhood! Who knows; maybe I would have been a part of the Tribute to Marian Anderson on her upcoming 80th birthday.

* * *

THE DAY PLYMOUTH MADE NEW YORK CRY

After floating around in the rain for forty-five minutes trying to locate New York Boulevard, because no one in New York remembered to tell the drivers that the name of the street had recently been changed to Guy Brewer Boulevard, the buses arrived at Calvary Baptist Church, Jamaica, N.Y.

It was 10 a.m. Saturday, March 12. As the passengers unloaded from the buses from Plymouth, they entered a basement area of Calvary, where family members and members of the North Carolina Club of Calvary waited to welcome and greet them. A very warm and moving moment. It was as if, after a long journey, the travelers were being greeted in heaven by family and friends who had gone on before them and prepared a place for them.

After the handshakes and hugs and kisses, the travelers were seated at prepared tables and served a breakfast of orange juice, eggs, grits, bacon, sausages, hot rolls, jelly and coffee; after which a rehearsal was held in the sanctuary until approximately 1:30 p.m. At this point a few people were taken to their hotel and the remaining choir members departed with their family or friends for a much needed respite, or whatever; to return to Calvary at 9:45 a.m. Sunday morning.

Upon arriving at Calvary, one encountered a massive traffic jam due to the fact that there were no vacant parking spots surrounding the church, and their private parking lot was filled to capacity. The church was crowded with Sunday School attendees.

Members of the New Chapel Baptist Church of Plymouth were directed to a basement area where the ladies changed into their long black skirts and white shirts, with black bow ties. Their luggage was stored in the same area until after church service.

The usually crowded church was really packed that morning. The special seating area set aside for the North Carolina visitors was grossly underestimated. We were jammed in and the church was hot.

Service began at 10:45 a.m. Plymouth's choir came in proud and tall, with heads reared back, and singing their hearts out. Looking good, too. And sounding great.

They were followed by girl scouts of all sizes, since it was not only North Carolina Day at Calvary, but also National Girl Scout Sunday.

Service continued with the usual preliminaries, including having everyone from North Carolina to stand (those now living in NY, plus those now living in NC). A great many of us stood up and looked around to see who we could see. Some of us hadn't seen one another for over forty years.

There were introductions and presentations concerning the scouts; and two collections. New Chapel kept rendering selection after selection, and the audience kept amen-ing them to death.

The preliminaries took so long that at one point Rev. Robinson left the pulpit. But he soon returned and eventually the dais was turned over to him. I do believe it was about five minutes to one o'clock.

In all my years, I have never seen a minister have everyone in the church crying before he even started to preach. He cast a spell on everyone. Not a dry eye in the place. He had all the deacons come forward with their wives, and had them all join hands. He had his family members in the audience come forward with the deacons. He prayed over them. The choir sang. One lady got happy standing there holding onto her deacon husband's hand.

Next came the treat of the day, the icing on the cake, so to speak. Rev. Robinson's three daughters sang two selections, as a trio, accompanied by their mother, the organist; but who was now at the piano. Such display of family talent and togetherness was very touching and heartwarming-- a rarity these days. Almost brought the house down.

The sermon began. "The Reward of the Faithful;" the story of Joseph, the son of Jacob and Rachel; Joseph, with the coat of many colors.

Rev. Robinson knows how to tell a story. Keeps you sitting on the edge of your seat; even if you know the story already. He has a way.

At the conclusion, a love offering was taken, for Rev. Robinson. Three offerings in one service! But Rev. Robinson sure deserved it.

It was a long service, but who cared!!!!

After the service, the reunion. People milling all over the church, as well as all over the church grounds. Little clusters of people joyously greeting one another. And as one walked around, inside or outside, people could be seen peering at one another, trying to see if they recognized someone from years past. And if they did, screeches of joy could be heard. If they didn't, they gave a smile and a hello.

It was a glorious day. All was right in the world. The sun was bright in God's heaven, and the temperature had warmed from Saturday's forties. But even had it still been raining, it would have been a beautiful day. And Plymouth was responsible. You should-a been there!!

I'm told that the choir was served a delicious dinner after church, and before boarding their buses for the return trip. My only regret was that I couldn't hang around to wave them off because I took guests home to my place for dinner.

But, to New Chapel; accolades, kudos, plaudits, and congratulations for a job well done!

Note: This article was published in the Beacon, the Plymouth, N.C. newspaper, under Church News, on May 11, 1983, page 12.

A WINNER

He forwarded my plane ticket weeks ahead, after I accepted the invitation to visit Indianapolis (Nap Town) during their most exciting weekend of the year, the Memorial Day Holiday.

My plane landed at 10:30 p.m., Friday, May 27, 1983. As I exited the plane area there he was, leaning against the wall with a silly grin, and eyeing me as if he was pleased with what he saw.

First stop, an all-night restaurant, with a smoking and non-smoking section. Hadn't ever noticed that in New York. The waffles were out-a-sight, and just being with him was pleasant.

Next, I was driven through the Indy 500 area, so that I could compare the same area on Sunday, the day of the race. It was a carnival atmosphere, with lots of vans and campers vying for a space for the weekend; someone's yard, a tiny strip of land, maybe a parking lot; anyplace. There were loads of motorcyclists as well as many people on foot, just walking the strip along the stadium; many carrying their six-packs or drinking beer as they strolled along. A glimpse of the license plates made it apparent that these people had come from every corner of the US, and parts of Canada. The air was filled with excitement.

Next day the annual parade; and I became a kid again. I had forgotten how exciting a parade can be. There I stood, snapping pictures galore, and jumping up and down when something special caught my eye. I was tempted to approach the young black policewoman on duty to ask if I could get further into the street to get closer shots, but thought better of it. I strained to see how many blacks were actually in the parade and I was pleasantly surprised. I saw the mayor, the deputy mayor, Phil Harris, old-fashioned one-wheel cyclists, vintage autos, horses that looked like they were from the Budweiser commercial (followed by a poopah scooper no less), beautiful floats covered with beautiful gals, black and white and all the Indy 500 drivers who were going to do their thing the following day. All the while overhead floated the Goodyear blimp.

From the parade, we went to the Children's Museum, recommended as a "must see" by a co-worker. First thing I did was to seek out the merry-go-round, but didn't get to ride on it because of so many children on line. It was a beautiful splendidly decorated carousel, so pretty that it didn't look real.

The Hall of Science proved quite fascinating because it was full of hands-on experiments. It was fun. And it's so true that travel broadens one (physically and mentally, that is) because I saw a replica of Wes Montgomery Park at the museum. Didn't know that Wes was a native of Indianapolis. My physical broadening came when I had a Kahlua hot fudge sundae.

No, we didn't go to the race on Sunday. But at 11:30 a.m. we left home and drove through the same area that I had been driven through the night I arrived. What a flurry! What a thrill! We caught glimpses of the thousands of people sitting in the stadium, and we could hear the tremendous roar of the motors on the cars. But there were still many, many people milling around outside the stadium also. As we rode, we had the car radio tuned to the race. Suddenly, the announcer spoke of an accident occurring at the stadium. We listened intently to hear whether anyone had been injured. At that very moment, to our left, we heard the sound of cars wrecking. We looked. We were actually passing the same area where the accident was in progress inside the stadium. I could see the tops of the race cars and I saw the paramedic truck. Bet I saw more from my position than hundreds of people inside the stadium.

Next, we went for a long drive, where I was shown a great portion of the city. We browsed in the lobby shops at the beautiful Regency Hyatt Hotel, drove pass the area of the Methodist Hospital, ending up at a huge shopping center where I purchased a pair of blue pumps (sales tax only 4%). I was impressed by all the hand car-wash establishments we passed in our travel. And I discovered what could be New York's answer to the graffiti problem. In some neighborhoods I noticed that all the fire hydrants wore bright funny faces. I was told that this was done by the children. Very unique, very striking.

It was planned that we would be away from the house until 7

p.m. because we knew that traffic would not allow us to get back into our area until that time. We were staying only five miles from the race track. Finally, we headed for home, but couldn't get there. So we ate at a restaurant where we could keep an eye on the traffic. The race was over now and the streets had become a sea of vans and motorcycles and crazy people boozed up on beer.

When I look back, I'm hard-pressed as to whether the weekend was magic because of what we did, or was it magic because of the person who shared it with me; or a combination of both. Whatever; it was A WINNER.

* * *

REFLECTIONS

The call came at 9 a.m. "Mrs. Speer, Dr. Kim suggests that you come right over." I was in the process of dressing preparatory to performing my usual routine of spending the day with my mother. But now there was no time for makeup, no time to remove my curlers. So I grabbed an oversized beret, pulled on a warm coat and dashed over to the hospital.

As I reached my mother's room I was greeted by the doctor, who merely looked at me sadly and shook his head. As I entered the room there were four nurses around the bed. One nurse was a cousin of mine on my father's side. As they left the room one remarked "If you need anything for yourself just let us know," closing the door behind her.

Now, alone with mother I assessed the situation. The head of her bed was raised to its limit, so that her head was past the mid-point of the distance between the floor and the ceiling. She seemed to be in a deep, deep sleep and her breathing was terribly labored; each breath sounding as if it was her last. Attached to her was a stomach pump, intravenous tubes and oxygen.

There she lay. Had never gone to a doctor before in her life. Because she was afraid. She had wanted to await my arrival from New York before going this time, but I insisted that my cousin take her two days before. And, as I suspected, the doctor immediately put her in the hospital.

A simple proud woman she was. And though a high school graduate, she spent her entire adulthood in service for a Jewish family in her home town in the south, having only retired in the last five years. Thinking back, I guess she was considered a Nanny, having raised that family's two female children until they matured and left home. I was shocked to learn in recent years that mother didn't cook for them. It seems that the lady of the house did the cooking while mother did the cleaning, et cetera.

My father had married her when they were very young. And, according to my father, she didn't seem to have time to take care of me so he took me, bag and baggage, at age two, to his mother, who raised me until she died. I was 13 at the time.

Both my parents married different mates somewhere through the years, but I know for a fact that mother never stopped loving my father.

Although I moved to New York, never having lived with mother before or after my grandmother's death, in later years I did visit her on Mother's Day or at Christmastime. And after the death of her second husband and my second husband, both in the same year, we became very close.

Her complexion was a shade darker than my own and her face, though terribly pock marked, was a pleasant face, a good face . And she had the brightest, most sparkling eyes. Clear eyes, like the eyes of some birds I've seen. Only five feet tall and in her later years a size 18-1/2, she was known for her cute feet, a size five, pretty legs, and the way she sort of strutted when she walked. Her carriage exuded dignity and pride.

Her hair was grey now, mostly around the temples, and her looks belied her 71 years. Now she lay at death's door, her body riddled with cancer.

Strangely enough, she made an excellent patient; never wanting to disturb the nurses, only summoning them in extreme situations. And as ill as she was she was always pleasant. Her melodic voice was soothing to the ear.

Each day I would brush her hair up on top of her head and put on a ribbon to match her gown. And Clyde, the teddy bear I bought and named after her second husband, would be sitting close to her pillow. The nurses would always comment on the ribbon and on Clyde, too.

My reflections came to a halt now with a slight stir from her. I glanced at her face and saw that her eyes were now open and focussing on the ceiling. I ran to the far side of her bed to enable her to focus on me. And when she did, suddenly, screaming with joy, with her arms outstretched and lifting the entire upper portion of her body off the pillows, she grabbed me in her arms exclaiming that "God is good, God is so good!" She frightened me no end. Her grip was so strong that I couldn't free myself, not that I really wanted to. Ant all the while just one thought kept going through my head, "They'll never believe this," meaning the nurses who had left the room when I arrived.

The door to the room quietly opened and in walked the nurse who was my cousin. On seeing the turn of events, she hesitantly approached the bed with a startled expression. When mother saw her, she released me and hugged my cousin, who gave her a broad smile but then pulled away, fighting back tears, and left the room mumbling in my direction, "I can't take this!" Next thing I knew, all the nurses came fluttering into the room to look and see.
Someone called Dr. Kim. He came, looked at me and smiled. Mother went back to sleep, but now her breathing was much easier.

Although I had been spending ten hours a day at her bedside for the last 17 days, when this episode took place it was as if she hadn't remembered that I had been there all along, even though we conversed each day. She acted as though I had just that minute arrived from New York. It was as if she had been waiting to see me one last time. Here, I thought she was about to draw her last breath at any minute and lo and behold she came back to life and lived 15 hours more.

* * *

A FOUR WHISTLE FAREWELL

The tearful funeral ended. The sermon was a good one, directed especially to the three remaining offspring. As the procession neared the grave site in this small town, I saw a freight train up ahead, standing right across the highway. Luckily, we arrived at our destination before reaching the railroad track, so the train didn't interfere. But as the multitude gathered, sinking in the mud around the grave, under an overcast sky, midst the garden of floral arrangements; and after the last prayer by the minister; in the stillness of the moment I heard four little toots from the freight train. And as long as I live I will think of it as a farewell salute to my Aunt Helen Jeannette on March 23, 1985, at 11:10 a.m.

* * *

PINK PEARL EARRINGS

It was 11:45 a.m. when we walked into Mt. Nebo Baptist Church at 114th Street and Adam Clayton Powell, Jr., Boulevard (7th Ave.); just in time for the 12 noon service. It was beautiful inside. Not just the stained glass windows, but the people were beautiful, too.

On the far left-hand side was a group of whites, approximately 50 in number; a strange sight in the middle of Harlem. For the next fifteen minutes gospel music blared from the front of the church while people filed in looking for seats. The music was jumping and a few people got caught up in it all, throwing their heads back and flailing their arms. The organist was having a good time. We had no choice but to sit behind the last pew on the right, in chairs that had been added for the overflow. This really upset Mama Bea because I was visiting her church for the first time and she wanted everything to be perfect.

Just before the sermon began, the whites left. I asked Bea what was happening. She was quick to point out that they were all visitors from foreign countries; that a group attends her church every Sunday; they sit, listen and observe for about a half hour, and then go on to their next stop; and some without even a knowledge of the English language. I remembered then that I had noticed what appeared to be an empty tour bus parked outside as we had entered church. I found this interestingly exciting and only wished that I could have talked with some of the visitors to learn what impression they had gathered. But this was not possible. And I thought, if you can't visit a peoples' home, what better way to try to gain insight into them than to visit their church service.

We then occupied two of the seats vacated by the foreigners, but were still sitting near the door. Since it was so warm inside, the church doors were flung open wide. And the sound of a loud speaker could be heard drifting in, obviously from another church. I am told that the other church was two blocks away and that no one complains because the loud speaker had already resulted in many lost souls being found who otherwise would not go to church, and that the other church is working miracles with the so-called undesirables. I found the noise of the loud speaker very irritating.

Upon hearing the beginning of the sermon in the church where we were seated, I began to think that maybe I'd be better off listening to the loud speaker. I thought for a moment that I was back in a little country church in North Carolina. The minister was talking about the way some women dress, and calling them Jezebels. It just didn't seem appropriate for this Sunday.

The congregation started buzzing and glancing around at each other as if to say Why is he talking about this today!!?

But fortunately for the minister, the entire church didn't feel this way, because after the sermon and the alter call, at least twenty people went forward to join the church. Come to think of it though, maybe it wasn't so much the sermon as it was the solo by a man screaming into the microphone, "If I Could Hear My Mother Pray Again."

As I sat there straining to hear what was being said up front, I noticed that entire families were at church, from newborn babies to great grandparents; and that many people were carrying wrapped flowers, as if they had brought them to give to someone after the service. Traffic was heavy inside, too, with parents taking children to answer the call of nature. But some went so frequently, I'm sure the kids were playing a game.

It was time for the collection, and we had to "march." Being a Methodist, this always turns me off. But "march" we did. And as we marched, Bea suggested we keep marching right on outside, because the arthritis in her knees was beginning to bother her anyway.

So off we went to Bea's place, one block away; a rented room in an apartment of eight rooms. Fortunately, there are only two other people living there, thus limiting the sharing of the kitchen and bath. Her room is not just a room; it's a fascination. It's like going to your fairy godmother's house; clean, neat, attractive, homey and inviting. And almost everything you want or desire is contained within this room. Everything is there, but cleverly hidden away, camouflaged; tucked behind here, pushed under there.

This was our first Mother's Day together since she and daddy divorced, and we were both excited at the idea. We had set it up during the week. Neither of us wanted to go out to dinner, because the nicer restaurants do not accept reservations on Mother's Day, and we didn't want to spend half our time together waiting on line. So she was to make chicken salad and I was to make potato salad. But on Saturday we talked and she informed me that she would make everything.

When we arrived at her room, we made ourselves comfortable and sat talking for a while, but soon ended up in the kitchen where we raided the refrigerator and took everything to her room. From behind the draperies she produced snack trays, fine china, silverware, dinner napkins and glasses. We helped ourselves to chicken salad, potato salad, shrimp salad, cold steamed green peas topped with French dressing, sesame seed crackers, and sweet vermouth mixed with red wine. It was simply scrumptious. We both had seconds.

Afterwards, when everything was cleared away, we talked girl talk while golden oldies were playing on the radio. Then Bea pulled out three jewelry boxes; one from here, one from there, and one from yonder. And we climbed up on the the bed and went through all the boxes, piece by piece. The third box contained what I will call heirlooms, some still attractive, some gaudy. I inherited pieces from each box, right on the spot.

Suddenly, I remembered that I had been searching in stores from Plymouth, North Carolina, to New York for Pink Pearl Earrings to match a necklace of the same. I opened my mouth to ask Bea if she had any and said instead, "No; I've never seen you wear pink earrings-- you wouldn't have any." And she said "Wanna bet!!!?" Well, I now own a lovely pair of pink pearl earrings.

The spell was broken when we realized that daylight had vanished.

The toys in the attic were all put away, and to Queens I returned after a most unusual and beautiful Mother's Day.

* * *

5/85

FOR FATHER'S DAY, 1985

This is a poem to my father

whom I have loved for 55 years,
whose graceful, smooth, beautiful hands
bear witness to God's artistry;

whether Lou is creating art in the
barbershop or fashioning miniatures.

Round-shouldered, tall and handsome
I thought you a Black Clark Gable,
especially in the photo where you 're wearing a homburg.

A ready, wide smile - but sometimes a furrowed brow.
Easy-going. Extending a helping hand, almost to a fault.

A youthful spirit, a teller of tales, A self-made man.

True blue...that's you, Lou.

So, I write this for life,for love, so you'll know the score.

For you,
my compassionate loving father
Age 74!!!

THE MEMORIAL FOR CHARLIE THAT WASN'T

Dear Charlie:

You should've been there when we marched down the aisle at Mt. Hebron on August 4, 1985 at 4 p.m.; the Class of '47 and the class of '41. Yeah, Charlie, the Class of '41 was with us. We were looking good in our blue and white. The Class of '41 was looking good, too, but they weren't the Class of '47, if you know what I mean.

And you should've heard the music by the Pentacostal Temple Choir--heavenly music. Guess you know all about that now, huh? And talk about my little solo. Did you ever hear a singer who made people cry? Well, crying ain't never hurt nobody, has it?

And you should 've heard the sermon by the handsome, young, new minister. He kept marveling over how good we looked, to be the Class of '47, and we silently kept marveling over how cute he was.

But I'm sure glad you weren't there for the memorial for you. Bet you would've been just as upset and disgusted, and mad and embarrassed as I was when it turned out that it was a memorial for nine other people, too; some of them so long gone that their candles wouldn't even light during the candle-lighting ceremony. And seated in the congregation was practically your whole family, those from far and near, who re-arranged their schedules to coincide with this special Memorial To Charlie. I don't know who the rest of the class lit their candle for, Charlie, but I lit my candle for you!

What's that, Charlie? You say you were there but you got disgusted and floated out before the end? Did you say two beautiful chicks were waiting for you anyhow? You rascal you-- You'll never change.

Well, since you left so early, jus' wanted you to know that The

Memorial For Charlie That Wasn't, really was. Because who among your family and close friends could ever forget what happened at the third reunion of the Class of '47?

* * *

HALLOWEEN

The air was electric. And I was a child again, waiting for a parade. On Thursday evening, October 31, 1985 I played hooky from choir rehearsal and ventured down to Greenwich Village to see that much-talked-about Halloween Parade. No, it wasn't because I was brave but because I was accompanied by Roger, a Court Clerk, who legally carries a gun.

We weren't hungry after work, having attended a luncheon for a retiree, but after arriving in the city by subway, from Queens, we stopped at a French bakery where we had miniature honey buns and coffee and sat talking, trying to kill time. The parade was scheduled for 7 p.m. and it was now only 5:45.

As we sat, surrounded by all the festively decorated pastries, parents began to enter with their children dressed in bright, colorful costumes and faces loaded with makeup. Roger wanted to sit longer but I, thinking that I might be missing something, was anxious to get outside. We joined the overcrowded sidewalk of men, women and children on Sixth Avenue and 12th Street. With difficulty we made our way to 10th Street and walked to our left towards Fifth Avenue, the route of the parade. The street was blocked off entirely with wooden horses, vehicular traffic was banned, and there were policemen and policewomen all over the place. Both sides of the street were jammed with people, but we managed to get to Fifth Avenue, where we found metal gates blocking the curbs. We just made it through to cross 10th Street, heading south on Fifth Avenue, before the police closed the barriers.

Our original plan was to head for the Arch D'Triumph at Washington Square Park, but a few feet from the corner of 10th and Fifth we found an opening in the crowd so we staked our claim by standing as if glued to the wooden horses. From this spot we would be able to see everything. Roger kept looking at his watch and I kept telling him, "Stop looking at your watch and look at the girls." It was now 6:30.

To our immediate left stood an Oriental couple who snuggled up and kissed the whole time we were there. My Irish friend Roger said, "Gee, I didn't think that Orientals kissed in public." To our immediate right stood an elderly couple, obviously parade enthusiasts, with a blanket and a thermos. Directly in front of us, in the street proper, was a policeman. Every few minutes someone approached him inquiring as to how they could get across the street. He had no answers for them. We were actually standing underneath a scaffolding made of wood and steel rods. At one point a young girl climbed up on the steel rods for a better vantage point, only to be told by the policeman that she had to come down. She asked him why, and he insisted that she come down. In a cute, little voice the girl said, "Oh, please?" He still insisted that she come down. By now voices could be heard in the crowd yelling, "Shoot her, shoot her!" She came down.

As we stood, slicksters came up to people near us and said, "Excuse me, can I get through there?" People moved to let them through and as a result lost their spot. Even though we were standing on the sidewalk facing out to the street, many, many people were walking up and down on the sidewalk immediately behind us. And that was a parade within itself. I'd rather think that these people were in costume, too, but I'm afraid that this was not true for the majority of them.

Fifth Avenue and 10th Street is a residential area of swanky apartment houses. Several residents who obviously were just arriving from work couldn't get to their homes. They couldn't even cross the street. After much frustration a few managed to literally crawl through the wooden horses from the street side to the sidewalk, buck the crowds on the sidewalk and gain entry.

Suddenly, from around the corner of 10th Street came a police car, and everybody cheered. Could the parade be far behind? Then came six mounted policemen. Another ten minutes, and then a big noise went up from the crowd. As we looked to our left, there came a stunning figure strutting a tight-fitting gown, a flowery headdress and high heels. It sauntered up close to the fringes of the crowd, posed for pictures, bowed, turned in each direction and bowed some more; sat down on the ground, with its back to us, crossed its legs for more poses; then rolling over on its back with its legs up in the air, quick as a flash spread its legs wide open. It was a guy; and the parade had begun.

Now this parade was like none other. It consisted of mainly great processions of men, women and children in all kinds of costumes. There were only three groups of musicians; one Latin, one Calypso, and one with whistles. Those in costume either walked or danced by, some coming to the fringes to talk to the crowd, or posing for photographs, especially in front of the TV cameras.

The most popular participants were not dressed as witches but as brides and as the Statue of Liberty, under repair no less. One bride had long, stringy, grey hair and the wrinkles in her face made her look a hundred years old. One man was dressed to look like a lobster, all over. There was a huge framed picture of Mona Lisa with a hole cut out where her face would normally be and the person carrying the picture stuck his face in the hole. There was a statuesque white woman, in black face, dressed like Tina Turner, who walked over to us and said, "What's love got to do with it anyhow?" I can't remember them all, but here are a few others: Someone dressed to look like an ice cream cone with a cherry on top; a camel with four humps; a subway train consisting of several cars from which pairs of feet and legs could be seen underneath; people dressed like drinks, i.e. Bloody Mary, Martini, Singapore Sling, etc.; two tremendously fat ladies, one with tremendous boobs, the other with a tremendous buttock; an open coffin being pushed as a vampire walked alongside saying, "That's my bed;" a female flasher wearing only a black bra and black bikini briefs underneath a raincoat; a pregnant nun; people dressed to look like M & M candy; people dressed like all the different Coca Colas; people dressed like fish, like a turkey, like Superman, like Groucho Marx and his brothers; a steam-spewing dragon, a huge Iguana, a huge pineapple; and a man fully dressed in leather, like a member of a motorcycle gang, except that his rear cheeks were exposed. Many of the participants walked on stilts and several even danced on stilts, and they were quite good.

Some of the marchers carried protest signs, protesting the satellite missiles, the transportation of nuclear waste through the city, anti-abortion signs, ban-the-bomb signs, "vote-for" signs, etc., etc., etc.

After watching for an hour or so, and just when the parade seemed to bog down, Roger said, "Howya doing, El?" When I admitted that I was getting tired, he quickly said, "Me, too," and we left the parade. With quite a struggle we made our way back to Sixth Avenue, walked to West Fourth Street, and took the subway back to Queens. Gone was the electricity in the air and the child-like anticipation. There only remained a beautiful harvest moon.

* * *

But For The Grace Of God

There she sat all shriveled up, tied into a wheelchair, with her thinning grey hair brushed severely back, and with telltale crumbs of her dinner scattered all over the plastic bib around her neck. She stared at me for a good thirty seconds and then exclaimed, "Oh, my goodness," in wonder and with a puzzled look of almost recognition. I hugged Ruth and kissed her, and her expression relaxed into one of pleasure.

Seated at the cleared dinner table was a newcomer to me, for I had not visited the nursing home for many months. A distinguished looking black woman she was, who spoke as if she was well educated and, from the quality of her sweater, a woman of means. "What's your name?" I asked. She smiled and said, "I don't know about that." After I asked her a third time, she either finally heard me or decided to answer, saying, "Mrs. Brown."

As I sat there looking around the dining room or family room, Mrs. Brown kept whispering to me, while constantly looking over first one shoulder and then the other, " These white people are something! You know, they don't want us black people here. It's like a prison here. They only do this to the black people. They won't let us out. You see that woman in the chair right there? Well, if they bring in a sixteen-year-old boy and sit him next to her, she'll get pregnant."

Odd that Mrs. Brown would say that about Marian because as I looked at Marian, who was strapped into a regular chair, she was moving her lower torso in a fashion not unlike a form of masturbation. I remember when Marian and Ruth were roommates. Marian would lay down on her bed for two minutes, get up, walk around the third floor for about three minutes, return to the room and lay down again for two minutes, and would repeat this routine all day. Now she was grounded.

As I glanced further around the room I recognized several residents. I waved to a short little graying black man who seemed to recognize me. The white haired, Irish-looking blind lady was still there. She used to hum and sing all day long. But this evening she was noisily complaining about her knitting and her neighbor upstairs. The nurse kept telling her, "You're not at home, you're in Wavecrest Nursing Home."

One resident balked at having to take her medication. And after the nurses succeeded in getting her to take it, she spent the next forty-five minutes waving her arm and patting one foot as if she was conducting a choir or an orchestra, from a sitting position, switching from one arm to the other, as one would tire I suppose.

I asked Ruth of the whereabouts of Elizabeth, another long-time resident'; whether she was still there in the home, and Ruth told me that Elizabeth had died. Moments later, when I walked away to wash a tangerine that I brought for Ruth, I saw Elizabeth at the far end of the room. She was in her usual state, hunched into one corner of her wheelchair with her head hanging down on her chest, her eyes closed, her mouth open, and looking so lost and alone and forgotten.

Over in the corner, also in a wheelchair, was the lady with the loud, strong, booming voice who intermittently yelled something in Italian and then slapped her hands together, one very loud clap, while several other residents yelled "Shut up!"

Ruth suddenly blurted out, " I don't understand why my sister doesn't come to see me." I was dumbfounded.

"Ruth, how many sisters did you have?"

"Just one, Juanita;" the answer I expected. I stared at her and said, "Ruth, Juanita is dead."

"What??! !" she cried. Then after a short pause Ruth continued:

"Well, she's been calling me up and talking to me every Saturday. She was getting ready to go away someplace."

"Ruth, Juanita has been dead for almost ten years."

"No!" she exclaimed. "Well, she's been calling me." Then, leaning forward, Ruth said to Mrs. Brown, "She says my sister is dead." To which Mrs. Brown replied, "You've got to watch these white people. You can't trust them." Ruth, still leaning towards Mrs. Brown, repeated, "She said my sister is dead." Mrs. Brown said, "We're in Prison."

"You mean you don't remember that Juanita died?" I said.

"No, I didn't remember."

"Ruth do you know me? Do you know who I am?"

"I remember your face, but I don't remember your name." She stared at me and the realization finally stung me that Ruth was really lost.

"My name is Eleanor," I said.

"Oh, yes;" holding her head back and still staring at me in disbelief.

"Do you know your name?"

"Yes, my name is Ruth."

"What's your last name?"

"I'm Ruth Gill."
"What's your maiden name? Do you remember?"

"My maiden name is Ruth Gill."

"No, that's your married name. Try to remember your maiden name."

"I don't remember."

"Wasn't it Edwards?"

"Oh, that's right. My maiden name was Edwards."

"Well, do you remember Juanita's married name?"

"No, I don't remember."

"Do you remember your birthday?"

"No."

"You were born April 4, 1907, Ruth."

"I was?"

"Yes." And, I continued, "Do you know that today is the last day of 1985 and that tomorrow will be the first day of 1986?"

"It will? No, I didn't know that."

"Now Ruth, believe me when I tell you that your sister Juanita is dead. I know where she's buried. She and my husband are in the same cemetery."

"Your husband is dead, too?"

"Yes, Ruth. He died two years after Juanita."

"And you live alone?"

"Yes, Ruth. And the lady who calls you every week must be Alice. Isn't it Alice? She's the one who used to always call you after church every Sunday. Are you sure it's not Alice?"

"She said she was my sister."

" But she didn't tell you her name was Juanita, did she?"

"No, she said she was my sister."

"Don't you remember Alice who calls you every Sunday?"

"We have a family friend named Alice, but she doesn't call me."

"I'm sure it must be Alice. I'll give her a call when I get home and I'll let you know for sure."

"All right. Well, I'm certainly glad you came to see me. You should come more often, so I can get myself straightened out."

I sat with them silently another ten minutes or so. After I put on my hat and coat, I pushed the bag of bananas in front of Ruth saying, "Take this to your room when you go."

"No, I don't think I want it. You take it back."

I turned to Mrs. Brown, "Would you like some bananas, Mrs. Brown?" She frowned. Then after the expression of indecision left her face she finally said, "No, I don't think so."

I put the bag in Marian's lap because from past experience I knew that Marian would take it .

"Marian, here are some bananas for you."

"Oh, thank you. I'll share them with the girls," Marian responded.

On my way past the nurse at the front desk, I mentioned that I had given the bananas to Marian because Ruth didn't want them and the nurse commented, "Ruth will probably want them back now."

As the elevator descended, I remembered that Ruth had gone through a period of not eating because she thought there was something in the food.

Oh well.............But For The Grace of God..................

* * *

THE UNFORGETTABLE KNIGHT

The call came at 7:30 p.m.

"Mrs. Speer, this is Mr. Lewis. I'm just leaving Manhattan now. Will 8:30 be too late?"

"No, I'll be here. Just ring my bell and I'll buzz you in."

At 8:20 p.m. the downstairs bell rang and I buzzed the door. The bell rang again and I buzzed again. The bell rang still again. Then I realized that the intercom must be out of order. I said a little prayer that Mr. Lewis would just enter the main door when someone else entered and come on upstairs, since he did call and I said I'd be home.

My phone rang.

"Mrs. Speer, I 'ring' your bell and you don't answer. I'm getting very annoyed."

"Mr. Lewis, I owe you an apology. I was not aware that my intercom was out of order until you rang. Please forgive me."

"All right, Mrs. Speer. No problem. But what shall I do now?"

"If you will return to the front door and enter with whomever enters, I'd appreciate it. And if no one enters in five minutes, please ring my bell again and I'll come down and let you in."

"Okay, Mrs. Speer." I quickly checked myself in the mirror, concluded that I looked like hell, but nevertheless slipped on some walking shoes, grabbed an old jacket, my keys and my mace in readiness in case he rang again. In three minutes my bell did ring again. I dashed out of my apartment, locked the door, hopped on the elevator and, when I reached the ground level, ran down the hall towards the front door.

Now I live in the last section of a three-section building. And as I neared the middle section I saw people in the hallway turning their heads behind them as they walked in my direction. As I drew near the front section of the hallway I noticed the object of their curiosity.

I saw the figure of a tall black man in a fur coat the length of which was just below his knee, a broad-rimmed dark hat, and carrying a briefcase in one hand and a large white box in the other. The figure had been coming in my direction but suddenly turned around and headed to the front section of the building.

"Mr. Lewis?" I yelled.

"Yes, my dear," he replied with a slight Jamaican accent and turned towards me. We had never met in person, but I knew he had to be Mr. Lewis, the furrier.

As we walked to the elevator, he with his quick, short steps and me breathlessly trying to keep up, I could see that he wore a black mink coat, a black hat, and several rings on each hand. I couldn't apologize enough for the confusion with the buzzer, and he kept telling me to relax. There was a third party on the elevator, a person that I did not know to be a resident, and I felt uneasy; what with Mr. Lewis' mink and his jewelry. But Mr. Lewis very cleverly drew this person into our conversation and the two of us arrived at my door safely.

We entered my apartment. He removed his hat and, with a flare, flung his mink onto a chair. He sat down on the couch, crossed his legs, adjusted his eyeglasses, and ran his hand through his greying beard. I couldn't help but notice his expensive pin-striped blue suit, his sky blue shirt with a solid white collar, his yellow print silk tie and his shiny black boots.

"Would you like something to drink, Mr. Lewis?"

"Yes, thank you; something very light."

"Riunite okay?"

"On the rocks, please."

As I handed him the wine and as he talked away, I tried to figure his age. From his thinning grey hair and slight pot belly, I thought him to be about fifty.

Mr. Lewis, how can you walk around, especially at night, with all that jewelry exposed, and with that beautiful mink coat? Aren't you afraid somebody will mug you?"

"Mrs. Speer, I have three cars and I don't walk; I use a taxi. He calls for me at my house every morning at 8:30. He takes me to the Long Island Railroad, and in seventeen minutes I'm in Manhattan. I have a BMW, a Cadillac and a Malibu Chevy. My neighbors only know about the Malibu Chevy because that's what sits in front of our house. The other two stay in my mother's garage. And everything I have is in my mother's or my wife's name. Nothing in my name. I haven't worked with Jews all these years for nothing. And if someone mugs me, they can have everything I have. I'm a lover, not a fighter. I'll just make a little phone call; I have lots of Italian friends.

"You see, Mrs. Speer, I'm 48 years old and I love myself. I came to this country 28 years ago with fifty cents in my pocket. I now have a degree in management, a degree in psychology, and I just opened two more fur stores."

"Really? Where are your new stores?"

"One in Detroit, and one in Chicago. You see, Mrs. Speer, I love nice things. I'm a Virgo and an only child. My mother raised me properly. I'm a mama's boy. I have good manners and excellent taste. My boots are from Italy, $185; my suit is custom made. I love jewelry. I treat myself good. I'm a workaholic. That way I can spend two months in Europe each year, alone."

"How long are you married, Mr. Lewis?"

"Nineteen years. I have a grown son and a daughter. They're out of the house now. There's just me and my wife."

"Does your wife help you in your business?"

"No, my wife is a dietitian. She goes to work at 4:30 in the morning."

"So the two of you don't see much of each other, do you?"

"Well, we see enough. My wife is very beautiful. And she's neat and clean. Like you. She's also a good cook. She's from Virginia. She's a very black woman. I don't like white women, I like black, but very black women. And I like noses. She has a gorgeous nose."

I had called Mr. Lewis who had been recommended by a friend, to come pick up my nutria fur coat with the blue fox collar for repair. Also, I had a friend's mink jacket and hat for glazing. The coats were laying on a chair across from where Mr. Lewis sat.

"Put on your coat, let me see."

I put the coat on and spun around a couple of times, so he could see.

"Mrs. Speer, you're a very beautiful woman. You need a mink coat. Why did you purchase a nutria?"

"Mr. Lewis, I know what I am, and I do not want a mink coat. At least I wouldn't buy one for myself."

"Why not? I'm not trying to make a sale. I don't need the money. I'm not rich, but I'm very, very comfortable. But you are neat, you're clean. I see your apartment. You're listening to classical music--You need a classic mink coat. Who sold you this nutria? And didn't he tell you that nutria splits in the seams?" "Well, maybe I'll sell the coat."

"This coat is worth nothing. How old it is?"
"Five years old."
"I'd give you more for the collar than the coat."
"Never mind. Will you just repair the seam under the arm, maybe put in a gusset?"
"A gusset? What do you know about gussets? Are you a furrier?"

"No."

"I'll give you a gusset under each arm."

"Fine."

Mr. Lewis poured another glass of wine and I noticed he spilled some on the table. I thought him unsteady.
"Mr. Lewis, would you like a cup of coffee?"
"Mrs. Speer, you hurt my feelings. Do you think I'm drunk? I'm a Virgo. I always know what I'm doing."
"Well, no. But I know all about Virgos, Mr. Lewis."
"Why Mrs. Speer, you are a Virgo?"
"Yes."
"Ahaaa, you're a Virgo," getting up from the couch with a broad smile, taking my face in his hands and kissing me on both cheeks.
"You're a Virgo, too!"
Sitting down again, he continued: "I was at a cocktail party before I came here. I drank a little champagne. But I'm not drunk."
"Okay. I just thought a cup of coffee might be in order. Sorry. Didn't mean to offend you."

As I wiped the wine off the table, I noticed the ruby among the rings on one hand, and the huge star sapphire surrounded by diamonds among the rings on the other hand.

"Oh, what a gorgeous star sapphire you're wearing, Mr. Lewis."

"You should see what I have on under my shirt," he said proudly. And before I could stop him he pulled his tie aside, unbuttoned the top of his shirt and fumbled and pulled out several gold chains, plus a chain with a gold medallion the size of a silver dollar.

"And, Mrs. Speer, I have $1500 on me, cash, right now; in my boots, in different pockets;" all the while reaching into his pocket and displaying so many neatly folded hundred dollar bills that it looked like an accordion.

"Please, Mr. Lewis, I don't want to see any more. I'm a nervous wreck just knowing all this."

He caught me glancing at my watch. "Am I keeping you, Mrs. Speer?"

"Well, I do have some chores to complete."'
"My taxi will be downstairs at 9:15. Is that okay?"

"That will be fine. I suppose I'll have to go down with you to help carry all this."
"Yes, thank you. In this box I have a red fox coat for a lady in South Ozone Park. I have to deliver it tonight."
"You're taking these two coats to her house?"

"Oh, no. I go home first, drop these two off, and then the taxi will take me to her house."

"How many fur coats does your wife have?"

"Mrs. Speer, my wife would be insulted by that question."
"Why?"

"Because she doesn't need a fur coat. All she has to do is tell me what she wants to wear at any given time. And if I don't have it, I borrow a coat from another furrier. Simple."

At 9:12 p.m. Mr. Lewis donned his coat and hat and I accompanied him downstairs, carrying the two coats he was taking from my house. I didn't really mind. At least this way I would know personally whether he had gotten out of my building in one piece. And also, I was curious to see if a cab was really waiting for him.

As we arrived at the front door Mr. Lewis stepped outside, lifted his hand in the direction of a car sitting just slightly past the main entrance. The car backed up to where Mr. Lewis stood. Mr. Lewis must have read the expression on my face, so he whispered in my ear, "Always owe them money, and they'll be waiting for you every time;" referring to the cab. And the Unforgettable Knight vanished in the darkness.

In all the conversation, Mr. Lewis neglected to give me a receipt for the coats; and I was so happy to be rid of him that I had forgotten, too. I called his office the next day.

He answered.

"Mr. Lewis, you're not very business-like. You're a disgrace to your mother."
"Who is this?"
"This is Mrs. Speer. You have the coats and I have no receipt."

"Oh, darling--you so sweet. I send the receipt out to you today. Let me have your address again. You know, Mrs. Speer, you have white eyes, lovely white eyes. I was telling somebody about your eyes today. Next time I see you, I seduce you--those eyes!"

"Mr. Lewis, you are crazy. Just send the receipt, please." All right, darling; I do it today."

Five days later, still no receipt. I called his office again and left a message after I was told that he was out of town. Later the same day I received a phone call in my office from Mr. Lewis. "Mrs. Speer, I'm in Philadelphia. I had to deliver a white mink coat to a customer. I send the receipt as soon as I return to the office."

A week later, still no receipt. I called his home and his wife informed me that he was out of town again. I left a message. Two Sundays later I called his home again. He answered. I said, "Mr. Lewis--" Before I could continued, he said, "Ah, Mrs. Speer, I sent the receipt. Didn't you get it?"
"No!"
"Well, your coats are ready. I'll deliver them Wednesday night.

Three Wednesdays later I stayed home from work to have my intercom repaired and to have some plumbing work done. I called Mr. Lewis'-- office and left this message: "Tell Mr. Lewis I will be home all day and all night, and that my intercom has been fixed!" Late that same afternoon Mr. Lewis called and said he'd deliver the coats that evening.

Around 7:30 p.m. my apartment bell rang and there stood dapper Mr. Lewis in an imported trench coat, bareheaded, and complaining bitterly about the cab driver. It seems that the cabbie had charged him $3.50 for a trip that should have been only $3. The removal of his raincoat revealed a beautiful medium brown sharkskin suit, a solid color tan shirt and a dark brown silk print tie. He immediately asked to use my phone and he called the cab stand. I overheard him complaining about the driver and stating that he never wanted him again; and that the driver shouldn't threaten Mr. Lewis because Mr. Lewis would "take care" of him. And when he hung up he turned to me saying, "You see, Mrs. Speer, it's not the money; I just don't like people trying to play a game on me."

One sip of a scotch and water on the rocks and he seemed to calm down. "Mrs. Speer, do you wear contact lenses?"

"No, and let's not talk about my eyes anymore."

I tried on both coats and everything was just fine. He did a beautiful job on both. And as he accepted my check I noticed a large square shaped diamond ring on his left hand that I didn't recall from our first meeting. He still wore the star sapphire on his right hand. And his polished, dark brown shoes looked like they cost a fortune.

When he finished his drink he requested to make another phone call and I jokingly said, "Okay, as long as you don't call China."

"Mrs. Speer, you hurt my feelings." Do you think I would do that?"
"Just kidding," I said.

He called the cab company again (He always uses the same company, he said), this time requesting a cab. And ten minutes later, after informing me that the next day he would be in Baltimore displaying several of his furs at the Ebony Fashion Fair, all expenses paid, he kissed me on both cheeks and had the nerve to give me several of his business cards. And for a second, and last time, this Unforgettable Knight vanished into the darkness.

* * *

VALENTINE'S DAY

Imagine a sea of people, say about 18,000, sitting in rows of chairs arranged in a circular position, sectioned off in different colors, with an opening in the middle of the circle, the arena, where all sorts of sports activities are taking place at the same time, i. e. jumping, high jumping, pole vaulting and track running; judges and officials milling around looking very distinguished in their black ties and red carnations; television cameras and cameramen, photographers, pages and messengers.

Now imagine sitting in the fourth row of the loge section, right in front of all the action, right where the pole vaulters run towards you and vault almost into your lap; where, when they make it over the crossbar they soar like an eagle and when they knock down the crossbar they look like a duck just shot out of the sky, and where a man rides over in his little mechanized lift, is handed the fallen crossbar and replaces it at heights up to 20 feet from the ground; but when the vaulting pole falls in the wrong direction, like on the track while runners are competing, your heart jumps into your mouth for fear the pole won't be removed before the runners reach that spot; where, when before the pole vaulter starts his sprint you hear an official say "Shhhhhhh" and not a sound can be heard from the 18,000 people until he vaults; where one official seems to stand on the track itself and as the runners approach him or pass him by he seems to be poking at them, and then you learn that he's only holding up fingers to let them know how many laps they have left to run, and he's really just standing to the side of the track.

Imagine also, after a rather long women's relay, the legs of one young thing, who has maintained the lead for many laps, turn to rubber and one of the officials takes her in his arms and lays her down on a cushion until she is able to get herself together. And the winner of still another relay reappears moments later for an interview in front of the TV camera with a baby slung over her hip.

Got the picture? Know the place? Yeah, Madison Square Garden.

And if your name is Eleanor Speer, that's where you spent the evening of Valentine's Day, 1986, along with Willie and Tommie, Carolyn and friend, Liz and Elmer, and Roger; eight little soldiers, all in a row.

Of course there were people of every color, but I have never seen so many handsome black men in one place before. And unfortunately for me, most of them were accompanied by beautiful black women.

It was a friendly crowd, lots of camaraderie. And from conversations I overheard, this was due to the fact that most of the people attend each year and they always sit in the same seats. For instance, the group I was with had watched the ten-year-old boy in the row in front of us grow up, because his parents had been bringing him since he was about four years old.

When the evening came to an end and we made our way down the escalator to exit the building, I counted twenty bag-people, male and female, black and white, bedded down for the night on the cement floor in a corner of the street level of this huge combination structure we know as Penn Station and Madison Square Garden. I couldn't help but stare. Finally, Roger touched my arm and we walked out into the snow.

* * *

RETREAT

Here I stand, waiting to be picked up at the Pittsburgh Airport. Edi promised she'd be here when I arrived. And it isn't like her not to be here. Something must have gone wrong. A half hour later, and I'm still waiting. I go to the phone and dial their home in Sewickley. No answer, of course, because normally at this hour she'd be at the shop. I dial the shop and ask for Edi.

"No one here by that name."
"Is this a florist owned by the McNeill's?"
"No. You must have the wrong number."
"Is this 7418082?"
"Yes, but it's not a florist. What's the name of the party you're looking for?"
"Edith and Henry McNeill."
"Sorry, but the name of the people downstairs is Jackson."
"I'm sorry to bother you. Thanks."

Now how could I do something that dumb!? I must have transposed a number. Let me walk over to ground transportation and see if Edi is waiting in her car. But I don't know the color or the make of her car. Well, maybe she'll spot me. No, that won't work. She knows my flight number and the arrival time. Surely she'd come to the baggage area. So I'd better stay close. Be calm girl, don't panic. Better get a plan in my head, just in case no one comes to meet me.

First, I'll call Information to see if I can get the correct number for the shop. Golly gee whiz, I don't know the name of the shop, but I know it's also in Sewickley. And if they didn't name it McNeill's Florist, I'm in trouble. And if this doesn't work, I'll check into a hotel until they get home from work and then I'll call the house and curse them out. Just kidding.

Back to the telephone, put on my glasses, getting ready to dial Information when who walks into the baggage area but Henry. Still can't figure out who was happier to see whom. It seems that he had been riding around the airport making wrong turn after wrong turn, and finally got permission to park in an illegal area. Then he walked around and walked around in the main terminal. Anyway, after almost an hour from the time my plane landed, I was rescued. Henry took me directly to the shop, where Edi was waiting with open arms.

The shop. That's what they call their florist/greenhouse/nursery. It's a little dream shop attached to a huge garage that houses Henry's giant Mack truck, the van for the florist deliveries and a pick-up truck. The combination building is tucked at the foot of a hill on a service road of Route 79, bounded in back by the 22-acre McNeill Forest; on one side by the nursery and on the other side by two houses and a quaint old Catholic church with glorious stained glass windows.

In front,on the other side of the little paved country road, there is a narrow stream of clear running water. And from the far side of the stream the ground rises to a hill so high that the traffic on the highway cannot be seen from the shop, except for an occasional top of a truck.

The office is filled with charm and warmth and love, not to mention some especially beautiful arrangements of silk flowers, plus exquisite arrangements of driftwood and silk flowers, and colorful live plants scattered here and there.

When I stepped from the office into the greenhouse I was immediately awed by the beauty of all the potted plants, some hanging, some not, some of bright, vibrant color; some I recognized, some I didn't. As I stood there with my mouth open, a feeling of well-being permeated my very core.

Henry drove me up to the house, maybe a half mile away, where I changed into slacks and flat shoes. Then back to the shop where, five minutes later, Edi had me figuring out a sale on a calculator, looking up the sales tax and giving change. It turned out to be fun, and I learned many things; one of which is that I can't count. But I did all right. Didn't really want to get "fired" my first day on the job! When there were no customers, I had a ball taking pictures all over the place. This was Friday, May 23, 1986.

On Saturday Edi showed me how to water the plants in the greenhouse, so that became my first duty each day upon the opening of the shop. Next, I picked all the dead leaves off the plants. In fact, Saturday morning as I picked leaves off the flowering plants, I talked to them and told them how pretty they were and that they would be sold that day. And as luck would have it, three of them were sold that very day. I thought I had discovered something!

Sunday was a slow day. Edi attributed it to Hands Across America and decided that she and I would leave the shop at 3 p.m. instead of 6 p.m. And off we went in search of new batteries for my flash attachment for my camera. And even though I'm "off the wagon," so to speak as far as ice cream is concerned, we ended up at a Baskin & Robbins across the river. My cone of praline and cream was the best ever. When we reached home, around 6 p.m. Henry, who had stayed at the shop to work on his truck, informed us that a few sales came in as soon as we left.

Later Sunday evening we feasted on giant crab legs at a Red Lobster about eight miles from the house. And when we dragged our stuffed bodies back home we sat around the kitchen table and I laughed my head off listening to Henry's and Edi's tall tales. I laughed so hard and so long that next morning I had no voice. True, true. Couldn't talk above a whisper. Back to the shop Monday morning at 9 a.m. where I did my little chores, took care of one sale, and before I knew it it was time to head for the airport for my return to New York and the mean, nasty, pushy, real world again. My Retreat had come to an end. And I thought to myself how lucky I am to have a place to escape to whenever the spirit moves me!

* * *

(Excerpt 1985 Reunion of The Class of 1947)

As our bus was entering Elizabeth City, N.C. an announcement was made that we would be making a brief stop near the Holiday Inn. No one paid much attention, just kept chatting away. A few minutes later the bus came to a stop in the parking lot of a beautiful one-story building. Then everyone wanted to know what was going down.

We were told that one of our classmates wanted to stop to see her mother, just for a minute or two. Several people became very upset because we had to be in Plymouth for our afternoon church service and we were pressed for time. But when word reached each passenger that Arnolia was going to see her mother, several people left the bus and paraded behind Arnolia.

As we entered the door, we found ourselves in a family-room type lobby filled with residents, most of whom were in wheelchairs. A voice could be heard saying, "Somebody's got a surprise!" We smiled and spoke and waved, but kept following Arnolia down a wide hall until we came to the right door.

The door was pushed open and there was Cousin Rose, fully dressed, standing at her closet with her walker nearby. She turned and looked in our direction and smiled. And oh, what a smile! A smile that should have been captured by my camera which I had foolishly left on the bus .

We each took turns hugging and kissing Cousin Rose and making her call our names. And she passed the test with flying colors, only halting or hesitating on one. But on that one she said, "I know you're Calvin's wife." This was truly remarkable because Cousin Rose hadn't seen some of us for many, many years.

Of course she wanted us to stay. But we couldn't. When we returned to our bus, two more people went in to see Cousin Rose because she had asked about them. And as our bus was turning around preparing to pull off, who did we see coming through the front door of the nursing home but Cousin Rose, on her walker. And as long as I live I will always be able to close my eyes and see Cousin Rose standing at the curb, smiling and waving us good-bye.

* * *

SUMMER '86

After waiting an eternity for my luggage to appear on the carousel, the beginning of my second visit to Los Angeles found me saddled with a Mexican taxi driver who, after driving me to my hotel, went out of his way not to touch my hand as he handed me my change, after I had paid the fare plus a mandatory $2.50 supposedly for the taxi to leave the airport. And were it not for my strong objections, he would have left my luggage in the middle of the roadway. So much for the Ugly American even in America.

The Summer National Bridge Tournament was an exercise in futility for my partner Eleanor Gill and myself. (In the bridge world in New York we are sometimes referred to as "those bad Eleanor's", a misnomer if ever there was one.) Two days before the tournament was to end, the posted final score sheet showed that we had tied for first and second place the day before, which meant we would be entitled to a trophy. (Everyone wants to win a National trophy). On the very last day we discovered that there had been what is called a protest period; that the scores had been changed and we had been pushed down to tying for second and third place, which means no trophy.

On Saturday afternoon, when I headed for San Francisco, after the tournament, with frustration permeating my whole being, I told myself that I would give up tournament bridge forever!

But all this flew out of my head when I saw Jem. There he stood, all coordinated in red and navy, waiting for me at the Frisco Airport with a rental car, having himself only arrived from New York an hour or so earlier. Off we drove, over California's magnificent freeways, to Vallejo, located north of Frisco, near the Napa Valley wine country; where we spent a week with Jem's nephew and the nephew's wife and daughter.

Their cottage, surrounded by flowers, was situated in a small community nestled near the foot of rolling hills, where the view changed moods innumerable times between sunrise and sunset but the serenity was ever present.

Sunday noon found me in a church that was perched dramatically on a hill, with my hostess and her daughter. Before the service began, the minister requested that we take the hand of the person in front or in back or alongside of each of us and to form a circle and pray together either silently or out loud. There were four in our circle. After I prayed my little prayer I looked around and listened. There were many circles all over the sanctuary, and the emanating sound was like people "speaking in tongues." Fifteen minutes later the service started "with a joyful noise" made by a piano, an electric bass, a guitar, drums and a choir of mixed voices. The music was lively, energetic and soulful , and by now the church was filled with young and old black and white. And almost everyone was very physical, keeping in time with the beat of the music. One young white couple in front of us kept jumping straight up and down like they were dancing at a disco. Everyone seemed to be having a good time, but at 2:30 we left. We had had enough.

On Monday we visited the Sterling Winery in Napa Valley, located on a hill so high that we had to take a cable car up to what looked to be a former monastery, a building sparkling clean and white and surrounded with very colorful flowers. The entire setting was out of The Sound Of Music. En route we passed the famous Christian Brothers Winery, but they were closed in order to make their building more earthquake proof, so I was told.

After touring the winery and on our way back home we stopped at the Veterans Home of California, located in Yountville, where my hostess is employed in personnel. She left work earlier than usual and gave us our own private grand tour of the Home. We didn't cover the entire 750 acres of course but we did visit the new club that had just recently opened, with its spanking new unpainted wooden tables and chairs; where one of the old timers saw us sitting at a table with cans of soda and without a word he got up from his seat and brought glasses for the ladies. We passed the bowling alley, and we shopped in the PX.

There seems to be something for everyone at the Home: Ceramics, a wood shop, needlepoint, hook rug making, water and oil painting, VCR training, carpentry, a library, golf, swimming pool, horseshoe tournaments, old car shows, canine rooms (a new experiment to determine if Members' pets can be successfully housed and maintained in the facility), and a newspaper called the Observation Post. But what struck me most as we toured the Home was the friendly smile with which our hostess greeted each Member we encountered, be it in the different buildings or along the outdoor walkways.

Tuesday found us crossing the Golden Gate Bridge heading for Sausilito, across the bay from San Francisco; a quaint avantgarde village not unlike New York's Greenwich Village or Chicago's Old Town, or Newport, Rhode Island. After a terrific seafood dinner in the outdoor garden of one of the nicer restaurants, we strolled along the narrow streets, window shopping, and ended up in a building called the Tree House, which consisted of four or five levels of nice little shops. And at the center of each level we found that we were outdoors, surrounded by trees, and when we looked up we looked into the sky. In one shop I purchased a soft yellow beret that had been marked down and when I came out Jem was watching a female caricaturist at work. He insisted that I sit for a caricature, and I did. I discovered how hard it is to smile broadly on command. And when I saw the finished product I wanted to ask, "Who's that?!" The remainder of our trip was spent in warm togetherness with our host and hostess. I had forgotten what it was to go to a drive-in movie. And I didn't realize that bingo was so sophisticated. Also, I observed a critical decision-making process involving a beautiful, well-mannered young lady her last night at home before going off to college in Louisiana. She and two of her dear girlfriends had been involved in an auto accident not caused by her but by the driver of the other car. No one had been injured. Her car was damaged and could not be used without a repair job. The conversation was between the father and the daughter. The mother was a silent pillar of strength. Her glances or non-glances were loud, but really non-committal to a stranger. The daughter was pleading her cause and doing a fine job of it (in fact, I think she'd make a terrific lawyer). The father was doing great too, but whatever he said she came back with sound reasoning. The bottom line was that she wanted permission to now take the family car and continue her last night out on the town. She won. And he won. He gave permission; she took the family car. The girls went back out, had a good time and came home in the wee hours safe and sound. Oh, the trust, the faith, the respect, the love!

At the end of our week, we bid a sleepy farewell to our host and hostess and at the airport we surprisingly were upgraded from coach to business class on a 747. We sat in two oversized seats just two rows in back of first class. Before take-off we were given a choice of plain orange juice or orange juice and champagne. After take-off we were given a printed menu with a cover picture of Pan American's first passenger flight, Key West, Florida, to Havana, Cuba, January 16, 1928. Next, we were asked to choose a libation and then to choose our entree of chicken or beef. Everything else on the menu we received automatically: First, hot rolls served in a basket, a delice fleurette salad of smoked Nova Scotia salmon with spring salad on a bed of fresh greens; beef brochette served with rice pilaf, buttered green beans and grilled tomato/or roasted chicken served with butter browned potatoes and a medley of garden vegetables; chocolate torte, rich chocolate cake baked with layers of butter cream filling; and a choice of twelve different non-alcoholic beverages, hot or cold. And I mustn't forget the cocktail nuts.

If this sounds like we were living high, you should have seen what was going on in first class. As the passengers arrived at their seats, their attendant took the men's jackets and hung them on hangers. Their drinks were served in fancier glasses. And a special dessert cart was wheeled to each passenger for the creating of their dessert, i.e. freshly scooped ice cream of all flavors, with any topping they desired.

By the time our luxurious service was over and the movie ended we were landing at Kennedy Airport.

No, this was not the end of a dream vacation. It continued a week later when we found ourselves on the road to Newburgh, New York, on the Saturday before Labor Day; where Jem left his car at my cousin's home in Newburgh and we ventured off with her and her husband in their camper which sleeps six. The camper is lovely and comfortable, like an apartment on wheels. We spent the night at Camp Ashaway, on the borderline of Connecticut and Rhode Island, where we hooked up to the camp's water and electricity for the night, and early the following morning we drove on to Newport.

In Newport we lunched on an extraordinary New England clam chowder at an outdoor restaurant, did a lot of shopping in the little shops, then back to the camper and toured Millionaires' Row. Later we watched fancy kites being flown in a meadow near the seashore. And at the foot of the bridge leading to the mainland we ordered seafood dinners from the take-out area of a crowded restaurant and converted the living room of the camper into a dining room. This reminded me of being in the dining car of a train, except that we were parked, of course. (I just love eating on a train). After dinner, when we tidied up, the fellows lounged while we took over at the controls. I was the co-pilot. But about thirty miles outside of Newburgh the driving was turned over to me and I brought us on in. It was a weird feeling dragging the weight of the camper.

Three weeks later found me the guest of Mr. and Mrs. Simon of St. Albans, Queens, New York, in their time-shared condo at Daytona Beach, Florida, for one unforgettable week. Picture this: 7:15 a.m. walks along the Atlantic Ocean trying to capture the sunrise with my camera; chasing sandpipers along the beach, sandpipers that walk so fast and smooth that they look like a mechanized children's toy; watching the pelicans flying in graceful formation against the sky or skimming over the water, diving for fish; watching the dolphins bob up and down in the ocean (first time we saw one someone yelled "A shark!" and we scrambled for our lives); watching schools of tiny, tiny fish at the edge of the water trying to avoid us as we tried to avoid them when we went for a dip in the ocean; nighttime walks along the beach to watch the moon rise; talking with the early morning or late night fisherpersons who were catching blue fish here and there(one lady caught a soft shell crab, but told us she was returning it to the ocean because the crab was covered with eggs. She turned it over to show us and the color looked the color of an old dried orange peel. Funny looking eggs!); lounging in the sun in the middle of the day, taking a dip in the pool or the ocean whenever the sun got to be too much; playing a hand of bridge at poolside now and then; reading The Day Of The Jackal at poolside; dining at a rustic seafood restaurant where a little old man who looked like Mr. Magoo played golden oldies from a book of giant print which told him which notes to finger! on a two-keyboard organ while, at our table, our group of ten played Name That Tune and then sang along, harmonizing no less; a one day visit to Epcot Center in Orlando, where we covered eight countries, and an ocean drive to Palm Coast, Florida, to visit the IT&T "ideal" community.

The day I returned home from Florida I visited my father and stepmother. Dad took one look at me and said, "Are you wearing 'black' makeup?" When I told him no, he shook his head and said, "Well, how on earth could you get *THAT* BLACK!!?" I don't think he appreciated my suntan. Even so, if I never have another vacation-- Got the picture???!

* * *

AND ON, AND ON, AND ON

It was Friday, July 10, 1987 at 11:45 a.m. and Inez and Sy and myself were heading for the 55th Street Pier to board the SS Galileo for a weekend jazz cruise to nowhere. JEM was to meet us there. Boarding was to be at 1 p.m. and we would sail at 3, so we were informed. Sy dropped us at curbside and parked his car on the roof. He then met us inside the pier where there was a crowd waiting to board ship. Inez and Sy hooked up with Willie (female) and Juanita and joined the waiting throng.

As I sat on my suitcase waiting for JEM near the entrance to the pier, trying to read Malcolm X, it was like a fashion show, watching the people heading for the gangplank. Little did I know this was only the beginning and that the entire cruise would turn into a fashion show, males and females, fat and skinny. In the middle of my people watching JEM arrived, gave me a big kiss, and off we went to board ship. The photographer snapped us as we started up the gangplank with Elaine, our hostess, joining us for the photo. A steward showed us to our cabin on A-deck, which was quite nice, even though whenever we flushed the toilet, we were afraid that we would get sucked in, too. It was like flushing on an airplane, only this seemed a hundred times more powerful. We quickly hung our clothes and went exploring.

We wandered through the Burbon Street Casino into the Olympia Ballroom that was about to overflow with people. There we ran across Inez and Sy with a group of other friends. They were munching on goodies and, seeing the look of hunger on our faces, directed us to the embarkation buffet on Promenade Deck. There we saw the famous singer Etta Jones eating with friends and relatives. JEM and Etta Jones, longtime friends, kissed (European style) and Etta waved to me saying, "Gee, I didn't know I was going to see you. I have something for you, but I didn't bring it with me." Everyone turned and looked in my direction, and I was so proud to have a celebrity yelling this to little ole me across a crowded deck.

JEM and I Joined the buffet line and, while snacking, the loud speaker announced that Houston Person and Etta Jones would be performing at 3:30 p.m. in the ballroom. We gulped our food down and rushed into the ballroom. There were no seats left, but a group of strangers made room for us to sit with them. One young lady made sure that we all introduced ourselves to each other, but I only remembered the names of one couple, Rudy and Delores.

Before I sat with the group, I spotted Brian Clark from Ron Anderson's Band, one of the groups performing on board. I sat next to him for a minute and experienced a nice warm feeling when he laid his head on my shoulder for a second and said, "Gee, it's good to see you." We spoke for a few minutes, mentioning how we both missed the Clark family singers (no longer together), of which we both had been members. Brian sings and plays the guitar, and his father is on the keyboards with Ron Anderson.

By now Houston Person's group was sounding good. And the audience was caught up in the sounds. When Etta came on to sing, it was like icing on an already delicious cake. She was in great voice, and the entire audience was all hers. Midway through the show someone glanced out of the window and exclaimed, "We're not moving!" Yes, we hadn't even started to sail. In fact, as we boarded, we were given a schedule of activities for the day which stated that sailing time would be 4:45 p.m. The ship was so smooth that when we did start to sail, no one noticed.

After the show I had occasion to go to the ladies' room in the bar that was just aft of the ballroom. It was a tiny room, and I found three ladies already there. As I stood waiting, I said out loud to no one in particular, " I can't understand why I'm seeing double." And a voice came back, "Because there are two of us, that's why." I was being funny, but there were twins, in there fifties I guess, wearing clothing approximately size 44, and dressed alike no less. The first day they wore pink turbans, white slacks, pink tops, pink socks and white low-heel sandals. Each day they dressed alike. They were elevated to celebrity status, what with so many people taking their picture and joining the twins to have their own picture taken. I had occasion to sit near them for one show and I observed that one twin was very quiet but the other seemed to be a swinger who didn't bite her tongue, and threw in a curse word here and there.

Later we dressed for dinner. The second sitting for meals had been chosen for us, and were we pleased to find that our table for six included Inez and Sy and Willie and Juanita. Our waiter was recognized by Sy as being the same waiter of two years before when they had taken this same cruise. And because of this coincidence we just knew that our time in the dining room was going to be great. But he turned out to be the slowest waiter in the dining room, maybe in the world.

After dinner we returned to the ballroom, where we danced until it was time for Joe Williams to sing. Our seats were so far away that we had to strain to hear him. And at one point I found myself nodding, so I took myself to bed. It had been a long, lively, fun-loving day.

Seven-thirty Saturday morning found JEM and me out on the deck with our cameras. In no time at all we were engulfed in clamminess and there was nothing to be seen except the ship itself because we were surrounded by fog. So we took pictures of each other, the smokestack, and the empty chairs at the pool. JEM wanted to partake of the coffee and danish on deck but I persuaded him to wait for breakfast in the dining room.

We joined our tablemates at 8:30 for breakfast. And Sy mentioned to our waiter that we were the last to leave the dining room the night before because of the slow service, and asked if he couldn't do a little better, because we didn't want to miss certain scheduled activities. The waiter became slower and even got our orders all fouled up.

Time now to complain to the maitre d'; and so we did. But we received no satisfaction from him. He just kept saying that there was a long line in the kitchen. All of us had after-breakfast plans, and I was the last to leave the table. As I walked past the maitre d' he said,"So long; see you at lunch." And I said, "I don't talk to you, and I won't be here for lunch." At this, he got excited and wanted to know why I wasn't coming back for lunch. Well, by the time I finished with him, suggesting that I shouldn't even be talking to him but that I should be speaking to his boss; that our waiter was a disgrace to the entire ship; and suggesting that our waiter looked ill anyhow, the maitre d' said, "You'll have a new waiter at lunchtime." When I returned to our cabin, I had lost the lens cap off my camera.

At lunchtime we did have a new waiter. He said to us, in his thick Italian accent, "I'm good waiter!" And so he was.

After lunch I wandered into the casino where I invested $20 in a dollar slot machine. And after playing a very short time I stopped and counted what the machine had given me. I now had $45. So I cashed in my coins, and with my $25 profit used $17 to call my father and Dottie from the ship's radio room. And even had he not been very ill at the time, I would have called just for the novelty of having them receive a telephone call from the ship. The chief radio officer wouldn't tell me where we were located, just said, "In the open sea;" (After all, it was a cruise to nowhere, wasn't it????) but all three of us got a kick out of it anyway.

While at breakfast Inez and I had discussed entering the leg contest to be held at poolside in the early afternoon. Sy put his two cents in, protesting that the announcement only said "ladies." He threatened to go and complain that the men had been left out. As it turned out, none of us went to the contest. But later that evening, while watching Joe Williams, a lady sitting near me said that she had entered the contest and that there had been four men contestants along with several females; that a tall, stately female had won; and that the ladies had been allowed to feel the men's legs!!!

Saturday, after lunch, we went back to the ballroom to hear Etta again. And before she came on and while Houston Person and the group were playing golden oldies, Inez and Sy had the dance floor all to themselves. They were looking good, too. I was forever losing JEM to some of his buddies (He knew so many people on board) and we had gotten separated. When Inez and Sy stopped dancing I noticed them walk to the starboard side of the ship. I learned later that JEM had been sitting with them, but they were not within my view. I ended up sitting with a Court Reporter from Civil Court. She was with her hubby, her sister and a large group of friends.

After this show and before dinnertime we were invited to have champagne in the cabin of Cora and Touhy, friends of Inez and Sy, in celebration of Willie's birthday. This was scheduled for 5:30. After everyone drifted into the cabin of the host and hostess, there was Willie and Juanita, Inez and Sy, Liz and Elmer, Helen and Tim, JEM and Ellie, and Lossie. Then came joke-telling time, when I saw a side of Cora that I had never seen before. We had a ball. And after we toasted Willie and sang Happy Birthday, and the host and hostess headed for the dining room for the first sitting, JEM discovered that he no longer had his camera with him.

We rushed to the ballroom where he had been sitting. Different people were sitting there now, and said they had not seen a camera. We dashed down to the information desk, where we learned that a camera had been turned in but someone had already claimed it. It was now time for us to dress for dinner and we returned to our cabin with long, sad faces. But as we dressed, JEM reasoned that it was about time for him to buy another camera anyhow; that this one had been the cheapest Nikon, and that he could use a more expensive one. After he had just about talked himself into thinking that was the end of his camera, he switched into a philosophical mood, pointing out that people are basically honest; about how he had left this same camera in a taxi in Jamaica, West Indies, and it had been returned to him; and he talked On, And On, And On.

As we were leaving our cabin to go to dinner, a lady walked up to us and asked had we gotten the-- We thought she was talking about the camera, but no, she was talking about my lens cover. She said she had been looking for us; that she had found a lens cover right outside our cabin door and that she had given it to our steward, assuming it was ours because of where she found it.

When we arrived at the dining room and before reaching our table, Inez was frowning in our direction and waving for us to hurry. I didn't understand, because we weren't really late. I couldn't imagine why she seemed so annoyed. When I reached the table, she had JEM'S camera in front of her. JEM had been stopped by a buddy, on his way to the table. Inez was beside herself. I was flabbergasted; couldn't figure out how they had the camera. I placed the camera in JEM'S empty plate. He walked over, spotted the camera, and his face lit up, his mouth dropped open, he grinned, held both hands up to the sky and said, "Aw riiight!!!" Then Inez and Sy, both talking at the same time, explained to us how they came to have the camera.

It seemed that the camera was noticed on the seat next to a couple who had been sitting near Inez and Sy. They waited for the camera's owner to return to pick it up after realizing that it was missing, but no one showed up. The couple remembered Inez and Sy, especially from seeing them alone on the dance floor earlier, and figured that the camera might belong to one of their friends, so they decided to carry the camera with them to the dining room and look for Inez and Sy. They spotted Inez and Sy and turned the camera over to them. Sy jotted their name and cabin number down and told them that the owner of the camera would get in touch with them. I looked at the slip of paper and saw that the man's first name was Rudy. I didn't recognize the last name.

After dinner our entire table went to the movies and saw The Color Of Money with Paul Newman. But before we went, JEM and I went to the cabin of Rudy and Delores. They weren't in, so we left a note. After the movie ended and the lights went on, SY saw the couple who had returned the camera and, yes, it was the same Rudy and Delores that we had been introduced to that first day. So JEM thanked them and invited them to have a drink with us in the Fantasy Lounge. Having my lens cover and JEM'S camera both returned, yes, people are basically honest. The rest of the evening was spent drifting from lounge to lounge listening to some fantastic jazz.

We docked at Pier 55 on Sunday morning, and by 10:30 a.m. the two of us were motoring our way to Cape May, New Jersey, on the Garden State Parkway, to join a couple from Jamaica, NY and a group of their friends to celebrate the wife's 55th birthday on Sunday evening in Avalon, NJ, a few miles north of Cape May. They had celebrated at the Chalfont, in Cape May, the entire weekend but we were only able to make the birthday party.

Arriving in Avalon at 3 p.m. and thinking that we could spend the night at the same place where the party was to be held, we drove to the Whitebrier Inn. Immediately, we both felt that we were in Stone Mountain, Georgia, where the Klan hangs out. So after learning that the Whitebrier was only a restaurant, we ventured on the Cape May by way of West Wildwood, N.J. And after locating the Chalfont and announcing our arrival, and wanting no part of the Chalfont with no air-conditioning and no private baths, we took an efficiency apartment at the La Mer Motel right on the Atlantic Ocean.

We had been told what colors to wear for the party; black and white, and how to dress; fancy but not formal. JEM wore a black shirt and a white captain's suit with epaulets, and I wore a black, slinky Wilroy knit dress with a boat neckline, a bold white belt and large earrings, black patent leather shoes and bag.

As we entered the private party room, filled with music from a deejay and decorated with beautiful fresh flowers, we were greeted by out hostess, also in black and white. A waitress saw to it that we had whatever drinks we wanted all evening, compliments of the host and hostess.

We were about thirty in number and everyone was given what I will call a dance booklet with deep purple braiding, to which a purple pencil was attached, and which had the words to the song THAT'S WHAT FRIENDS ARE FOR printed on the back. This was to be for a game where the individual who collected the most names in their dance booklet would win a prize. What I liked most about the booklet idea was that in getting your booklet signed you quickly got to know everyone at the party.

A miniature copy of the menu had been mailed to each couple beforehand. And, sure enough, everything was there; buffet style. After dancing and eating and drinking for a while, we noticed that the hostess had disappeared. Soon afterwards, as the deejay started to spin a specially arranged HAPPY BIRTHDAY, our hostess made her entrance, looking very lovely in a short pink dress with a crenoline petticoat, pink shoes, and pink flowers in her hair.

At this point an exquisite wine glass was handed to each of us and at the appointed time it was filled with Martini and Rossi Asti Spumante, a favorite of mine. We then formed a circle around Vivian; several toasts were made, which we drank to, and then the deejay played THAT'S WHAT FRIENDS ARE FOR, and we sang along. And after Ed danced with Vivian, everyone else danced. While we were dancing, one of the waiters entered with a flaming birthday cake, which Vivian took care of in one big puff.

After this, the dance booklet contest was held, and the fellow who won received a folding lawn chair. We had been told, "No gifts please." But each guest received a gift; a grey box tied with grey ribbon. I only saw what was in my box and Jem's box, but I assume they were all the same. There was a fancy thank-you card signed by Vivian and Ed, tan and purple streamers, a split of champagne together with a plastic champagne glass; two cocktail napkins, one tan, one purple; honey peanuts, two packages of imported butter cookies, three lollipop bubble gums, a little straw like pouch stamped with the words, "cheap but nice," and party favors.

We danced until 2 a.m., then drove back to Cape May. Next morning at 11 a friend of mine, who resides in Cape May, met us for breakfast at uncle somebody's pancake house where we had the most delicious pancakes ever. She brought a package for me, which she said she had had for quite some time, and which turned out to be two sets of salt and pepper shakers; wooden coffee pots from Wildwood and two squarish shaped plastic shakers covered with gorgeous sea shells. Thanks to friends, my collection is forever growing.

Tuesday, when I returned to work, I felt that I had already had my summer vacation. But my vacation starts on August 3rd.

* * *

Epilogue:
A week later we saw Etta Jones perform at the 79th Street Boat

Basin, Riverside Drive, Manhattan, and she gave me a beautifully wrapped box, tied with yellow ribbon, and inside was a pair of "hatching chicks" salt and pepper shakers.

WEEKEND IN THE POCONOS

As the car was flying through the air, heading for a tree on the side of the road, her only thought was that God was taking her instead of her father who lay on his deathbed back in the city.

Twenty-five miles an hour, on a lonely country road, a dark, drizzly Saturday afternoon at 1:30. Into a curve, and suddenly no traction. They flew off the road into the woods; flew over a boulder and landed on still another. Missing the tree by an inch, the car came to a standstill.

The driver hopped out, ran around to the passenger side of his 1987 Coupe de Ville and started jumping up and down and cursing like mad. She sat perfectly still, observing that her seat belt had remained fastened. She moved her fingers and wiggled her toes, realizing in utter amazement that not only was she alive, but that she didn't even have a scratch. She felt that he, too, was okay because he was in perpetual motion, still cursing away. With no difficulty at all, she opened the passenger door and yelled to him, "But we're alive!" After repeating this a number of times, he seemed to calm down. At least the cursing ceased.

Fifteen minutes later, along came a stationwagon occupied by a little old white couple who returned Louise and Edward to the hotel. The bridge tournament was in full swing, but word spread very quickly that someone in the group had "cracked up" their car.

After notifying the Pennsylvania State Troopers and contacting a tow truck, they sat in their room in quiet wonderment and awe and thankfulness, awaiting a phone call for the next move. Eventually, the tow truck picked Edward up at the hotel and they went to the location of the car. Later, a friend took Louise back to the scene. Before the tow could begin to retrieve the car, boulders had to be removed with chains. And in attempting to dislodge the car, the tow truck fell apart. Louise and Edward did not await the arrival of a second tow, but returned to their Poconos resort.

Back at the hotel, the last evening of the bridge tournament, it was time to dress for dinner and look especially nice for the show afterwards at the nightclub. Edward said, "Why don't we just dress for dinner and let everyone see that we're really okay, and then return to our room and relax." Handsomely dressed, and en route to the dining hall building, they were practically mobbed by hotel guests inquiring as to their well-being after the accident and expressing their concern and happiness that they were both okay. As they entered the dining hall, they experienced the same thing. It was as if their near tragedy had elevated them to celebrity status. They could hardly wait to finish dinner and return to their room.

Five minutes into the room, and at 9 p.m. the phone rang. Her heart skipped a beat. Was this the call she dreaded and yet hoped for; the call telling that her father's dying without dignity was ended, the call that would herald the fact that he was out of his misery; the call signalling the end of her relationship with her best friend; the call tolling the end of a beautiful man, a wonderful man, a tall, handsome man; a warm and caring human being, a self-made man, a clever man, a gifted man, a man who managed to touch the heart of everyone he encountered; a man who never lost his sense of humor even on his deathbed; a man who was loved by all three wives even after he divorced two of them; a man who truly loved his daughter's step-grandchildren as if they were his flesh and blood; an easy-going man; a talented barber who took care of the haircuts for at least two generations in several families; a man who cut hair by appointment only when he had to work sitting down because of terrible varicose veins; a man who went to his disabled and/or aged customers' home or hospital bed to cut their hair; a man with the most beautiful hands ever, a man who made miniatures of anything you'd ask for, be it something comical or serious; a man who gave a helping hand to more people than will ever be known; a man with an imagination; a man who rarely attended church but was the epitome of The Good Samaritan.

Yes, this was the call. Her father had died at 8:15 that evening, September 12, 1987, on her 58th birthday. At midnight the night before, Edward had surprised Louise with a beautiful, gold designer's necklace and bracelet, a lovely card, and champagne.

Louise's father had been living with cancer of the prostate for sixteen years. It was only in the last five years that the quality of his life had begun to deteriorate. He had been in the hospital for just over a month at the time of his death. But on at least three occasions during this time it seemed that his next breath would be his last. And each time, on the very next day, he would perk up and become lively again. In fact, after one of these episodes that seemed quite severe, Louise's oldest uncle, Aaron, said to Louise, "I guess Louis must have found the water too rough and he came back!" So after the accident that Saturday, with neither Louise nor Edward receiving a scratch, and then Louise's father's death later the same day, Louise pictured St. Peter trying to get her father to let go of life and enter into heaven, and each time her father saying, "No, not yet; I'm not quite ready." She pictured St. Peter getting tired of her father stalling, and St. Peter saying, "Now, look! Once before, a few years back, you were scheduled to come up here but we had new employees at the time and they took your brother Thomas instead of you. But this time you're definitely overdue. And if you keep stalling, we'll just have to take your next of kin." No sooner were these words out of St. Peter's mouth when Edward's car went off the road. And when Louise's father saw that St. Peter was really serious, he yelled, "No, no. I'll go. Don't take my daughter! I'll go."

Louise felt that yes, even though her father lay in a hospital bed in New York City, in St. Lukes to be exact, he had saved their lives many miles away, back in Pennsylvania. After all, her father had genuinely liked Edward, and Louise had the impression that her father belived that he was leaving her in good hands.

Incidentally, Edward's car was totalled by his insurance company.

* * *

OCTOBER 30, 1987

The transformation took place in the front seat of the car. When it was completed, they exited the car and entered the lobby of the Astorian Manor Catering Establishment in Queens, N.Y. As they walked towards the Blue Room to attend the Bennett College Alumni Annual Dinner Dance (costumes optional), they could feel the stares of some of the passers-by and see the smiles on the faces of others.

The ticket-taker, looking askance, asked, "Whose guests are you," to which Louise replied, "Mary Boland's." One of the hostesses grinned, stealing a glance at their unusual wigs, and said, "This way, please." They followed her to Mary's table. Once Mary recognized who they were, her mouth dropped open, her eyes lit up, and her lips curled into a delightful smile and expression of disbelief. Louise and Edward removed their raincoats, revealing identical very short garments of authentic-looking tiger skins over one shoulder, with jagged edges. There was applause. Edward whispered to Louise, "Baby, we got them eating out of our hands. We have the first prize wrapped up!" Louise reponded, "Cool it, kid! Let's wait and see!"

When they got on the dance floor, remarks could be overheard to the effect that they were both bare legged and wearing hand-made, flat sandals; and that he carried a club and she carried a stuffed animal (which she was using as a pocketbook). Someone said, "His hair and mustache and beard cover almost his entire face. How can he see?!" "And look; they both have nice legs!" One lady touched the bottom of Edward's garment and wanted to know what was underneath. Louise threatened to hit her with Edward's club. In reality, Edward was wearing corduroy shorts underneath his tiger skin and the dressmaker had added a piece of the same fabric to the edge of the shorts.

It was obvious that they were the center of attraction on the dance floor. When they returned to their table they caught a glimpse of themselves in the mirror. Even they had to laugh. She rather liked her black wig, a sort of kinky-straight, uneven look, which stood out from her head, almost as if she had stuck a wet finger into an electrical socket. His wig, by contrast, was a straight texture and hung past his shoulders. His mustache and beard had the texture of her hair. In fact, they had switched wigs because he hadn't liked his.

At the end of the dinner, but before the serving of the dessert, the announcement came that it was time for the parade of all the people who were in costume. The judges were announced; the music began. They paraded: The skeleton, the skunk, the dancer with the high hat and cane, the witches, the devil, the African girl, the bunny, and the cave man and his woman, as they were dubbed.

As they were going their second time around the floor, out from nowhere came a lady dressed like a baby, in pink and white, crawling and dragging a huge baby bottle and a blanket; stopping now and then to sit on the floor and rock back and forth in time with the music, either sucking her bottle or her thumb, and then crawling again. The audience howled. Louise said to Edward, "I think we just lost first place," to which Edward mumbled, "Yeah, you might be right." The music stopped. The judges were ready. The drums rolled. Third prize went to the "baby." Second prize was given to the skunk. And the first prize went to--yeah--the cave people!

* * *

Epilogue: First prize was a bottle of Chivas Regal and a bottle of Spanish Champagne.

Anyone want to borrow two slightly used winning costumes???!

RIVER OF JANUARY

We had a late night snack, saw a movie, listened to several channels of music, had drinks, indulged in intermittent shut-eye, ate a full breakfast; and nine and a half hours later our plane landed in Rio de Janeiro (River of January), two weeks before Carnival. It was early afternoon, January 30, 1988, and the temperature was 98 degrees.

We boarded the tour bus, en route to our hotel, along with many of our fellow passengers who were to be dropped off at various hotels along the way. Shortly after leaving the airport, we encountered what seemed to be a traffic jam. After a few minutes of creeping along we came upon a Volkswagen bus turned up-side-down on the roadway, with people still inside and one woman lying on the ground all covered with blood.

First, we rode through poverty stricken areas, passing the exceptionally neat harbor at Guanabara Bay. In the distance we could see thimble-shaped Sugar Loaf Mountain, Rio's equivalent of the Eiffel Tower. And across from Sugar Loaf we could see Corcovado (Hunchback) Mountain crowned by its 120 foot high statue of Christ the Redeemer, whose arms are outstretched to welcome visitors to Rio. Before we realized it, we were riding along the beaches of Ipanema and Copacabana, where even I was dazzled by the beauty of the women. Actually, I think I was more dazzled by the scanty beachwear.

After riding through two of Rio's fifteen tunnels, we passed the famous houses on the side of the hill, houses that looked like stacked-up match boxes, houses of all colors; the same houses that slid down the hill in the mud when the rains came in Rio, the day after we returned to New York.

On we rode. Passengers were dropped off at many of the big hotels; the Rio Sheraton, the Rio Palace, the Nacional, the Intercontinental; lavish, gorgeous hotels. We passed the Mountain of the Two Brothers and spacious private homes. And when the grand tour ended we were in what I would call a suburb of Rio, at the Tropical, our hotel, in an area called Barra da Tijuca. It was four o'clock and the sun was still bright. It was a quaint little hotel, with the ocean for a front yard, and there were "Birds of Paradise" growing at the entrance to the building. When I say quaint, I mean quaint. I thought we were in the middle of a Humphrey Bogart mystery movie. Everyone spoke Portuguese. Only one person at the front desk knew a bit of English. And every time we asked him for something that he didn't want us to have, such as a key for each of us, he pretended he didn't understand what we were saying.

We took the tiny, dark, wood-panelled elevator to the seventh floor. Our door opened into a small, musty room with a table and two chairs and a refrigerator, which was loaded with beer, sodas, wine, potato chips and nuts. Adjoining this room was a small bedroom and a bath. In the upper portion of the bedroom window there was an air-conditioner. It looked like the skeleton of what it once was; all covered with dust and cobwebs, with several knobs missing and a piece broken off the front of it. There were two small beds, two night tables, one with a radio that didn't work, a television, a dresser, and adequate closet space. The bathroom consisted of a stall shower, a tiny, tiny sink with trickling water and no stopper, a toilet and a bidet.

After a painstaking telephone call to the desk, complaining that our air-conditioner was not working, there came a knock on our door. We opened the door to a man in work clothes, holding a screwdriver. I thought to myself, "Is he for real? Does he really think he can fix that relic with a screwdriver?" He spoke no English. We pointed to the air-conditioner. He tinkered with it for a few minutes and left. It was not working. At this point we decided to request a different room. So after a second painstaking telephone call, I guess it was the housekeeper who came and indicated to us that we could take the room next door on our right. As we gathered our things together to move to the new room, the air-conditioner came on, as if by magic. Later we learned that the air-conditioners were controlled from the front desk and that it had just been turned on. But at that point I thought the repairman must have been a genius to get that piece of junk to work at all. Our new room was a bit more cheerful and the air-conditioner looked a lot better than the other one, and it was working. Just as we finished unpacking, it suddenly became very dark outside and a big wind began to blow. We rushed to the window and saw trees bending halfway to the ground. People on the beach were scrambling to leave. There was a flash of lightning and a loud clap of thunder. Then the rain. Our lights went out. The air-conditioner stopped. Thank God, Jem remembered to bring a flashlight. About twenty minutes later the lights and the air-conditioner came back on. And Jem looked at me and said, "Everythang's gonna be awright!" And I felt reassured.

Funny, the day we arrived, we felt we had been banished to the other side of the tracks. But each day we liked our hotel more and more. And we were told that it was better to be out where we were than to be in the heart of town; also, that it was safer where we were, safer on the beach, safer at our hotel. Anyway, we took no chances; we just pretended that we were still in New York.

Ordering meals where there were no menus was a trip. There were no breakfast menus because our hotel and the neighboring hotels all served a buffet style breakfast of ham, cheese, rolls, butter, juice, fresh pineapple, watermelon, honeydew and papaya; and of course that famous Brazillian coffee. The papaya was served with its many dark brown seeds attached, which looked like bugs, but it was the sweetest and the most delicious of all the fruits. Jem wouldn't go near it. And the coffee, served in a cup not quite as small as a demitasse cup, was super strong but delicious (and I'm not even a coffee drinker). We brought back a few boxes but I'm sorry I didn't bring more. If you wanted something for breakfast that wasn't in sight, such as eggs, you could almost forget it. By the time you made them understand, or if they ever understood what you wanted, it could be lunchtime. Ordering dinner was much easier. There were menus, and they were in Portuguese and English.

One day we walked a few blocks to a grocery store. We wanted to pick up some snacks of our own choosing. This was a combination bakery, deli, meat market and grocery store. The fruit looked totally unattractive. The meat was beautiful (Rio is known for their beef). The groceries were familiar-looking labels but with strange names. The deli had odd-looking foods. And almost all the baked goods was covered with flies. No one seemed to notice but us. We only purchased a large bottle of soda and a box of packaged cookies. The local stores do not have bags. You carry your purchase in your hand. I did notice that there were bags at the big shopping malls.

We stopped at a post office to mail our cards and I noticed that people with boxes to mail had left them open. And as they reached the window, the clerk went through everything contained in the box, piece by piece. Fortunately, we didn't have to wait on that line.

One day we took the public bus into town. Their buses are unique in that each bus is manned by two men, one at the front and one at the rear. The one in the front operates the bus and activates the front and rear doors. The man at the rear sits in a little cubicle and collects the fare and activates the turnstile through which a passenger must enter to reach the seating portion of the bus. All passengers enter the bus at the rear. They exit only from the front door.

The bus ride was interesting, with everyone staring knowingly at us. A bridge player back home in Queens, who had recently visited Rio, had told me of a shoe store in Copacabana that had a big selection of leather boots in large sizes. Well, we found our way, by bus, and I hit the jackpot. I purchased two pair black boots, one pair taupe, one pair brown and a pair of black pumps. Jem said I was like a kid in a toy shop. And I only spent one thousand crusados all told, the equivalent, on that particular day, of $100 in our money. The rate of the money exchange varied each day.

One evening we had scheduled a tour that included dinner at one of the famous Churrascarias (restaurants known for their barbecued meats) and a show at "Platforma I" (equivalent to our nightclubs). A tour bus picked us up at our hotel at 7 p.m. It had been raining all day and it was still raining, but not a downpour. To our surprise, there were only four people on the bus; the driver, our tour guide and the two of us. It seems that all the other people on this tour were staying at hotels in town and they had already been picked up and deposited at the restaurant. We were heading into the heart of town when suddenly the bus could go no further. We seemed to be trapped between the ocean on one side and a mountain on the other, with water like a waterfall pouring down onto the roadway. The rushing waters had brought the traffic to a complete standstill with loads of little cars, mostly Volkswagens, scattered all over the two-way roadway in both directions. Many motorists abandoned their cars and asked to board our bus, but our guide denied them entry, explaining that we ourselves were stranded and thus would not be going anywhere. Upon spotting a familiar face behind the wheel of a Volkewagen bus, our tour guide removed his shoes and socks, rolled up his pant legs, and stepped out into the raging water to speak with his friend. A few minutes later he returned to our bus and very excitedly, in his careful English, explained that we had to leave our bus and get into the Volkswagen bus; that his friend would try to get us back to our hotel. "Are you coming with us, I cried!?" "Of course," he replied. Earlier, as we were dressing for our night out, I had put on a casual dress but wanted to wear heels and stockings. Jem took one look at me and suggested I take off the heels and stockings and just wear my flat sandals. I'm so glad I listened to him, because now we're on the tour bus about to step down into the angry water. No need to remove our sandals. Jem just rolled up his pant legs. As I reached the bottom step to exit the bus, our guide, standing outside in the water, took my hand. I stepped down. The water came to my knees. Jem was right behind me. The guide let go of my hand to help Jem. I held onto our bus for dear life and made my way to the Volkewagen, the front of which was touching the front of our bus. I was sure if I had let go, the water would have swept me along like a twig. Yes, even at my weight. As much as I dislike Volkswagen buses, I was so very glad to be on this one with Jem sitting beside me. He hadn't rolled his pant legs high enough, so he was soaking wet.

The Volkswagen bus tried to get us back to our hotel, but we only made it to one of the big hotels in the heart of town. Our guide sat us in the lobby of this hotel, saying that he would go upstairs and call his office to find out what they suggested. As we sat in the lobby I recognized a couple who had been on our flight. We sat and chatted with them (in English of course) until our guide came with the news that everything was cancelled, that we would try again the next evening; and that he would go outside and see if he could find someone who would be willing to take us back to Barra da Tijuca. Meanwhile, the couple, who hailed from Michigan, bought a round of drinks, complained how the husband's luggage had never arrived, complained how they got caught in the rain; introduced us to their airline pilot daughter, told us about how careful they had to be where they were staying as far as thefts, etc., etc. Shortly, our guide returned with the good news that he had located someone who would be willing to take us back to our hotel, for double the money of course. But who cared! And he again rode with us and saw us into our hotel. The next evening we were able to make the dinner and the show without any problems, although it was still raining.

This particular Churrascaria consisted of a large, plain room with long tables covered with white tablecloths. Different dishes of food were placed on the table, such as potato salad, artichokes, chopped raw onions with pimentos, rice, fried bananas, fried potatoes, and escarole. Then, a parade of waiters came to our side, each one holding a skewer with a different barbecued meat on it. First, they brought sausage, then beef, more beef, and more beef (all different cuts); chicken, pork, and more beef. They placed the tip of the skewer in each person's plate and stood with a huge, sharp knife and sliced away until the person indicated that they had enough. And just when one thought they had eaten a bit of everything, the parade started all over again.

After dinner we were taken to "Platforma I." Before the show started, about ten musicians stood in a straight line across the back of the stage playing native music. A tall gentleman from the audience, dressed in a leisure suit, walked on stage and began to do the Samba. Then he came back into the audience and was persuading members of the audience to get up on stage and dance. When he reached us, Jem and I looked at each other and said, "Why not!" By the time we reached the stage it was crowded. We, the only blacks, had a good time doing our "thing," but one female was so vigorous in her native-like Samba that I was afraid we'd get stomped on, so I suggested we take our seats. More people had arrived while we were dancing and now, seated next to us, was a young black couple from Boston, who was spending a week in Rio and then heading to Brasilia for a week. The show started. On the mezzanine level, to the left of the stage, there stood three men and three women, dressed very prettily and nicely made up. They did all the singing for the show. The instrumentalists were on the orchestra level, to the right of the stage. The show told the history of Rio, in song and dance, and all in Portuguese. But ah, the show girls!! The prettiest girls you ever did see. And ah, the costumes; the likes of which you never saw. And here, we finally saw native blacks that were not down trodden. Mostly all the dancers were black like me but tall and shapely, graceful and beautiful. What bodies they had! Almost everything was exposed when they were not wearing the big, beautifully designed costumes that their Carnival is known for. An indescribable, beautiful, breathtaking, extraordinaire, extravanganza it was.

Next day, while in town at H. Stern, South America's leading jeweler, specializing in all kind of stones, some English speaking tourists approached us and commented that they had seen us dancing the night before at "Platforma I." You should have seen us grinning.

H. Stern's World Headquarters is in Rio, and no tourist can escape. The minute we registered in our hotel a Stern's representative was there to register us, too, for a trip to Stern's. We were told the trip could be made at any time we desired. On the day we decided to go we notified our front desk. Stern's sent a car for us and they took us to a small Stern's branch located in a big hotel a few miles from their world headquarters. We were instructed to remain in the car. A lovely lady came to the car, confirmed where we were staying, and gave us a gift (a magic charm) and the car then took us to headquarters. Upon arriving at headquarters, another young, attractive female greeted us as we alighted from the car, and ushered us to their fully equipped gemological laboratory. The lab is all glassed in, so we saw everyone at work. We were given earphones so that we could listen to a lecture as we made the tour. A friend had asked me to look for her birthstone while in Rio, a Peridot. I was not familiar with Peridot, so I asked her the color. She replied, "It's a funny-looking green." After the lecture we were assigned a salesperson, a lovely Oriental middle-aged lady, and we went in search of gold hoop earrings for me and a Peridot stone for my friend.

Mrs. Chaing sat us down in plush seats, with a glass top table separating us from her. After discussing what we were interested in purchasing, she left and soon returned with trays of emerald rings and emerald stones exclaiming that the emerald was a better color green. After we insisted on seeing Peridot stones, she brought out what few they had. It was interesting to watch her change of attitude when she realized we were serious about making a purchase. She then ordered a young girl to bring us hot tea with fresh lime, which was served in clear glass cups and saucers with a sterling silver spoon. If the tea, which was excellent, was a psychological move or technique, it worked. The three of us relaxed and Jem had Mrs. Chaing actually laughing out loud. We purchased the Peridot stone. And when Mrs. Chaing asked, "Would there be something else," I inquired about gold Hoop earrings. She brought out trays of gold hoop earrings and I found a pair that I really liked. (The Peridot stone made a hit with my friend back home. It was exactly what she was looking for.)

When we completed our purchases at Stern's we were told that a car would return us to our hotel; but that if we wanted to shop in the area, we could; just to return to Stern's within the next three hours and their car would still take us back. And so we did, and they did. It must be great to always have a chauffeur.

It was during this little shopping spree that I noticed a few homeless people. Not as many as I see in downtown New York, but there were some. And only one lady with a small boy approached us, begging for money.

While in town we made a reservation to take a helicopter ride so we could take pictures of Corcovada and Sugar Loaf, among other sights. The ride was scheduled only for the afternoons, if weather permitted. After we made the reservation , it rained every afternoon.

When we went on the beach everyone really stared at us. Jem

thought he had it all figured out one day and said, "Maybe they think you're wearing a blanket," referring to my "regular" bathing suit as compared to the scanty "things" that everyone else wore. I didn't let the stares bother me though. I held my head high and pretended I was setting a style trend.

One day I walked one block, alone, to the next hotel, which had a little shop that resembled our drug stores (without a pharmacy). After I made my purchase, a gentleman whom I had not seen in the store on my previous visits, and who was behind the counter with the two regular girls, offered to drive me wherever I wanted to go. He spoke English. The girls did not. I thought it strange and of course I thanked him and declined his offer. When I got back to our hotel and told Jem what happened, he growled and made faces, saying "Where is he; let me at 'em!!" Then he said, "You haven't seen my jealous bag, have you?!" I laughed because he was really funny. He's quite an actor, but it made me feel good.

Whenever we were in our room we had the TV on. Every channel was full of Carnival; dancing, singing, colorful costumes. And everything was in Portuguese. But late one night, while switching channels, we ran across an old American movie, in English, with Portuguese titles. We were estatic.

To our dismay, the day we set aside to visit the Samba School it was closed. And this was a real heartbreaker, since we would miss the actual Carnival, where they dance in the streets for 48 hours. But hey, c'est la vie!

And so, our week in paradise came to an end. We had seen, smelled, tasted, felt, and definitely heard Rio. And it was grand.

* * *

THE ADVENTURE OF THE SUMMER OF '88

There we were, the three of us, on our way from Vallejo, California to San Francisco Airport heading for the Philippines. Gene (Jem's nephew), Jem and me. The flight was scheduled for 9 p.m., August 27, 1988. We arrived at the airport at 7 p.m., boarded the plane around 8:30 p.m., and at 2 a.m. we were still on the ground in San Francisco. "Mechanical difficulties" is what we were told. Several times we were invited to leave the plane and walk around; even served refreshments just inside the gate. Around 2:45 a.m. we were asked to board the plane again. And soon afterwards the loud speaker announced, "Ladies and gentlemen, I regret to inform you that there will be another fifteen minute delay." There were over 300 Filipinos on the plane, and we three. And in all this time we had heard no one complain except us, but only among ourselves. We looked at each other knowingly and then agreed that this was a job for "Super Jem." So off went Jem and Gene to seek out the Purser, who had been making all the announcements. Fifteen minutes after they returned to their seats the Purser announced, "Ladies and gentlemen, we cannot fly tonight. Please take all of your belongings and reenter the airport. We will be sending you to a hotel for the night. Please return to the airport by 2 p.m. tomorrow. Flight time will be at 3 p.m."

Next day we arrived at the airport at 2 p.m. and boarded the plane at 2:45 p.m. At 3:25 p.m., as we actually started to taxi to the runway, I happened to glance out the window and noticed one of the ground crew running urgently in the direction of the front of our plane. We stopped. We pulled back to the gate. And this is what we heard: "Ladies and gentlemen, we regret to inform you that we are having further technical difficulties. Please take your belongings and wait outside in the area of the gate and we will give you further instructions momentarily. This flight is officially aborted, so we have to make other arrangements. We will try and get you onto the 11:30 p.m. flight. Dinner vouchers will be forthcoming for the restaurant on this level here in the airport. We're very sorry to inconvenience you." No one complained. Shocked, yet relieved, we three were numb by now but we really didn't want to even taxi onto the runway in THIS plane. Philippine Airlines (PAL)! Is this why everyone looked at us sideways when we mentioned we were traveling on Philippine Airlines? Did they know something that we didn't know? This flight made the earlier flights by Jem and me, from New York to Chicago and then Chicago to Frisco, seem like a piece of cake. Our three days in Chicago were perfect. Precious time with family and friends, Sunday brunch, luncheon invitations, a visit to the Museum of Science (saw the Great Barrier Reef), and a little jazz.

The jazz was great, but the game of people-watching was even better. We sat in a booth that was raised from the level of the floor, giving us a good view of the rest of the club. Directly across from us was a long bar with several barmaids, one of whom really stood out in that she was the most attractive, the most popular, had the dirtiest mouth, and she was a chain smoker. Our barmaid, who wore a mini dungaree skirt and a lowcut top, approached our booth with a felt-type money bag on each arm. I had never seen this before. But one bag was the bank, for making change, and the other was the night's receipts. And I'm certain they weighed a lot more than she did. At the far right of the bar was a raised platform for the musicians. To the left of the musicians was the entrance door to the club. Our booth was the nearest booth to that door, so we could see people as they entered. Seated at the bar was an old guy pawing over a not-so-much-younger female. All evening. And during the course of the evening lots of men came into the club alone. Each one had on a hat of some sort, oddly shaped, as if each one was trying to outdo the other. Except for the Texas-looking guy, who didn't have to try, what with his ten-gallon hat and his boots with spurs. At one point a tiny, little female strutted in wearing a very skimpy, hot pink, one-piece mini knit that was so tight under her hips that she looked molded into the dress. At the same time a loudly-dressed male came from the back of the club and met her about mid-range of the bar. They seemed to be together. Next entered three big women. The shorter of the three, who wore a red sequins tassel dress, pulled up the right-hand side of her dress, exposed a well-shaped leg, and slinked over to the bar, in time with the music no less, and said in a loud, clear voice, "All right, all you mother fuckers, clear the bar and let me sit down." She looked over her shoulder and winked at Jem. Then she slinked over to Jem and, while revealing a closed switchblade knife in her hand, whispered, "I guess I told them, huh? They'd better not mess with me." When she finally sat down at the bar, while Jimmy Witherspoon was singing his heart out, she yelled, "Sing it, Jimmy; you handsome dog you. Here I am over here, honey." The taller of the three women who entered, the one with giant, red polka dots all over her dress, was later approached by the bouncer and she disappeared, never to be seen by us again.

Our three days in Vallejo, thirty miles north of Frisco, were comfortable, like a favorite old shoe. We caught up on a couple of movies, "Coming to America" and "A Fish Called Wanda," with Toy (Gene's wife) and Gene, and enjoyed a special dinner at Mama Soul, the most scrumptious soul food of the whole trip, as it turned out. Here it was the end of August and we were feasting on chitterlin's, corn bread, collards, potato salad and lemonade. We stuffed ourselves so, we had to take the dessert (homemade plain cake) with us. We spent one day in Frisco, where we remembered to get acquainted with our brand new video camera. Completely forgot to use it in Chicago.

At midnight on August 28 we finally left San Francisco on Philippine Airlines. Four hours later we landed in Honolulu, where we stayed for an hour. We continued on to Manila, arriving on Tuesday, August 30, having crossed the International Dateline.

The trip seemed to have been one long eating session. Every time we drifted off to a nice sound sleep, the attendants would wake us up to eat still another meal. After a while we lost track; couldn't tell whether it was breakfast, lunch, dinner, or just a snack!

The plane was crowded. And even though each person was allowed only two carry-ons, all the Filipinos carried on large, over-sized boxes wrapped in brown paper; boxes that were too large to fit overhead or under the seats. So they merely held them in their laps or put them directly under their feet and sat scrunched up for all those 15 hours. And as long as the passengers had their seatbelts on, there were no complaints from the flight attendants. The luggage that the Filipinos checked also consisted of these same type huge boxes. It looked as if every person was carrying half of the United States back to the Philippines with them.

Butch, our host (Gene's son) was waiting for us when we arrived. Our luggage was a long time arriving on the carousel. And I was sure the airline had left it on the aborted flight. But when it did arrive, in no time at all we went through Immigration and found ourselves riding in a four-door, white Mercedes taxi, which Butch had waiting for us, in the middle of heavy traffic filled with small cars and jeepneys, on our way to a hotel in the heart of Manila's financial district which, incidentally, looked as if it could have been the financial district of New York City.

Jeepneys originated as army surplus jeeps. The Filipinos stripped them down to essentials, lengthened the vehicle, reloaded it with rediculous accessories, decorated it with baubles and beads, or tassels and graffiti, placed a nickel stallion on the hood and a portrait of the Virgin Mary on the dashboard and then gave the vehicle a name like "Hot Stuff" or "Super Chick."

Butch had arranged for us to spend the night at the Mandarin Hotel and to delay the two-hour trip from Manila to Olongapo (the location of Subic Bay Naval Base, our destination) until the next day. He and Gene went on to Olongapo that evening. All of us, plus our luggage, could not fit into Butch's car anyway. Our little stop-over at the Mandarin was a God-send. My feet were so swollen from the trip that I didn't recognize them. So the very first thing I did upon arriving at the hotel was to have a massage and sit in the sauna. The hotel supplied a white his-and-hers terrycloth robe in the bathroom (a first for me), and when we ordered dinner through room servicve an entire table was rolled into our room.

Next morning we breakfast 'd at the Tivoli Restaurant in the hotel. It was like a movie set, with stained glass windows of garden scenes, and tremendous arrangements of fresh flowers as decorations. The waiters, male and female, were dressed in formal black and white. The tables were set with fine chinaware, heavy silverware, crystalware, linen-- you name it. My dry, decaffeinated coffee was served in a pretty glass dish with a silver spoon, so that I could make it as strong as I liked, with a silver pot of hot water on the side. Melted butter for my pancakes was served in a silver warmer. And there was a choice of two free morning newspapers in English. The national language of the Philippines is Tagalog, but everyone speaks English also.

By 2 p.m. we were in a van on the road to Olongapo. The midday traffic in Manila was equal to Friday rush hour traffic in New York City, but our driver proved to be an expert. The crowded city streets gave way to a two-lane toll road which brought us to a narrow, paved, two-lane country road, a road full of trucks and jeepneys, of trikes (a tricycle-type motorcycle with a covered seat built onto it) and school children and goats and buses and country people and slow-moving vehicles and fast-moving vehicles; where passing any vehicle turned into a game of "chicken" because you were in the wrong lane facing on-coming traffic that was not that far away from you. There were no sidewalks, no posted speed limits.

On either side of the road could be seen Nipa huts (native straw huts) and people working in rice fields or riding on a caraboa (oxen). Also there was a lot of smoke in front of some of the huts. I thought they were just burning trash, but I later learned, from Cynthia (Butch's wife) and Butch, that the smoke was from fires used for cooking meals. And no matter how poor the villages looked, there was always a beautiful church. We passed one cock-fight arena. This was truly the Road of Life.

While en route to Olongapo our driver pulled into the yard of a restaurant and announced that he had to pee. He came back in no time and we continued on our way.

Butch had told our driver to drop us off at a business located just outside one of the gates at Subic Bay and that he would pick us up there. The minute we arrived at the drop-off Butch drove up. It seems that he had been back and forth every few minutes to make sure he wouldn't miss us. We switched to his little red Nissan with our luggage. He showed his ID to the guards at the gate, and we were admitted. I heaved a sigh of relief because now we were on safe ground. A few minutes' drive brought us to a clean, neat, beautiful community of spacious private homes. And when his car stopped, we were in front of a high row of steps that led to manicured grounds of trees and flowers and bushes. At the top of the steps was an attractive, attached stucco house. It was only after we got out of the car that I realized how hot the temperature was. It felt like 110 degrees in the shade. After trudging up the many steps and entering the house we were hit by a most pleasant surprise-- air-conditioning. It felt like heaven. I don't know what I had expected, but this was my first surprise. Then I noticed all the conveniences of home more so than home. There was Cynthia, Butch and Gene, of course; Fiawna, their 13-month-old daughter; Lita, their maid; and another female busy cutting patterns on the dining room table. She turned out to be a seamstress.

When we entered the front door, we walked into a lanai, very similar to a built-in porch, which was furnished with heavy upholstered bamboo furniture covered with cheerful print fabric of old rose and white. And there was a stately grandfather clock of mahogany. The back wall of the lanai was open, like a big picture window with no glass, and looked right into the living room and beyond. Evidence of Cynthia's creativeness could be seen in every part of the house, and it was very impressive. Fiawna's room was a fairyland of bright and glorious colors, filled with all kinds of stuffed animals, from miniatures to giant size.

On our second day at the house I had something I'd never had before; a pedicure. Every other week a lady came to the house and you could have a manicure, a pedicure and a massage; all three for about $10 to $12 United States currency. The fellows had the works, but I was satisfied with a manicure and a pedicure. The seamstress came to the house once a week, arriving around 9 a.m. and leaving around 5:30 p.m. She would sew for all of us, and she received one payment of $7.50 US currency per day. She made two blouses for me and two shirts for Jem.

Going to the breakfast or dinner table became an adventure in itself because Cynthia pulled out all the stops. She planned all our meals to the Nth degree and her menus were so varied and attractive that one could not help but appreciate even the minutess detail-- not to mention the table settings. For example: Calico blue and white plates along with blue-handled flatware; white china seashell dishes; black bone china along with gold flatware; white bone china trimmed with pink and blue roses; tall, clear fluted stemware; stainless Danish flatware with cut-out handles; individual salt and pepper shakers of dark blue and silver; square, wooden plates; you-name-it.

Cynthia was substitute-teaching while we were there, covering a teacher who had an emergency, but she was always home by 2: 30 p.m. We usually ate a late breakfast, always planned by Cynthia but prepared and served by the maid long after Cynthia and Butch had left for work. So there really was no need for lunch. But one day Butch, who had to work the whole time we were there, called the house and suggested we call for a taxi and meet him for lunch at the Officer's Club at Subic Bay; and the three of us did. The landscaping at the club and the view from the club were both outstanding and beautiful. On one other occasion we met Butch at the club. He had told us to wear our bathing suits under our clothes because he would be dropping us off at the beach afterwards. So I wore thongs on my feet instead of regular sandals. When Butch joined us at the club entrance and we were heading for the dining room, I was approached by an officer who informed me that I could not enter the dining room wearing thongs. I insisted that I wasn't hungry anyway and said that I'd wait outside. Butch got upset and announced out loud that he would never eat there again. He had not known about this rule, and he was as embarrassed as I was. And from our first visit, we saw that Butch had loads of friends at the club. Anyhow, we grabbed a snack at a place close by and then piled into the car and Butch desposited us at the beach. And the warm water of the South China Sea, with the Bataan Mountains in the background, turned our afternoon into a glorious day. I learned later that thongs are the shoes of the poorer class in the Philippines. At the beach Jem and Gene swam like fish and I did my little floating-on-the-back number. There were only four other people on the beach!

We had found it strange that the few blacks that we saw on the base were not friendly. But while at the beach a "brother" walked by and spoke. And before he knew it, Gene had the guy cornered in conversation as we lounged in beach chairs. The guy was very young and talked like an expert in the field of flying military planes. In the midst of this very interesting young man's conversation I happened to glance behind us, and there stood Cynthia. She had come to take us home. This was how she and Butch took care of us the entire trip. One would take us and the other would bring us back. And whatever we wanted to do, they saw to it that we did it. We three, as visitors, could not shop in certain of the stores on the base. But Cynthia and Butch applied for permits for us to window shop. And as long as we were with one of them and we saw something we wanted to purchase, we asked them to purchase it for us and we handed them the money. Off base was an entirely different story; we could purchase whatever.

After the boys' first night out, I was told by you-know-who that the "territory bar girls" in Olongapo try to entice the men walking in front of their territory into their bar, and they try to do this before you pass their territory; and that they offer the men everything, including a free sample.

Sunday morning, September 4th, Labor Day Weekend, we five grownups, plus Fiawna, ventured off to Baguio (the summer capital of Manila), a mountain resort approximately five hours by car from Subic Bay. For this trip we rented a four-door Ford, and Butch did all the driving; his fast mad, crazy driving. Whenever we left Subic Bay to go any distance we always had to go by way of what I've dubbed the Road of Life. And on this Sunday morning at eight o'clock there were lots of people all dressed up, obviously on their way to church; and there were lots of church vans on the road. Sunday must be wash day, too, because almost every hut had a clothesline full of mostly children's clothing.

On we rode, passing the trikes and jeepneys and chickens and goats and children, horse and buggies, a truck full of pigs, ox-drawn carts and rice fields. After a couple of hours we parked at a restaurant and ate some of the goodies that Cynthia had brought along. Afterwards, everyone except me went inside the restaurant to have a soda or to use the facilities. I volunteered to stay with the car, which was full of cameras, plus the video camera, and also because I wanted to take more pictures. After everyone left me, a four-door white car drove up and parked next to our car. I was sitting in the back seat, holding my camera. The doors of the white car opened and two men stepped out, holding machine guns. I quickly hid my camera and looked in the opposite direction of their car. Four people altogether had alighted from the white car and they all went into the restaurant. Within the next few seconds my heart dropped at least a foot as I said a prayer that these people wouldn't shoot up the place with all my folks inside. Shortly afterwards, my folks came outside and my sigh of relief was a great big one. Butch said "Ellie, you didn't have to worry; I was inside!"

Now I know that Butch is good at what he does (Naval Intelligence) and he has a great rapport with the Filipinos; even speaks their language, but-- Anyway, that was a close call as far as I was concerned. Butch explained that one of the four men was the mayor of a nearby village and the men with the guns were protecting him as bodyguards.

On we rode, passing the area where Corazon (Cory) Aquino, President of the Philippines, grew up, as well as the area where the famous Death March took place. We crossed a bridge that had a sign "Danger Weak Bridge!" Were we supposed to stop, get out of the car and walk across one at a time; what? This sign meant absolutely nothing to Butch, for we crossed at the same fast speed as always. When we started the drive up the mountain, there were big bumps and craters in the road; a frightening, zig-zaggy road. We stopped to get shots of a picturesque waterfall as well as scenery that reminded me of the "Sound Of Music." Once in a while we would see a Nipa hut sitting in the middle of the mountain and I wondered how it came to be there. It looked impossible. And sadly, I noticed dried up riverbeds full of rocks. We passed a giant head of a lion carved in the mountain, with a sign that said "International Lion's Club." How any equipment got up that mountain road to carve the Lion's head, or to do anything for that matter was a puzzlement to me. I was marveling as to how we were getting up there. Good old Butch; he did a terrific job.

We finally arrived in Baguio, at the top of the mountain, where it was comfortably cool. I thought there'd be just a big resort hotel at the top, but to my surprise it was a thriving, bustling city with lots of jeepneys and hotels and people and sightseeing spots; an army base, the President's summer palace-- a tourist trap, really. We had Sunday brunch on the army base. Afterwards we decided to spend the night in Baguio to avoid being on that horrible road at night. We registered at a cheap-o hotel for the evening, hired a jeepney just for us, and went sightseeing and hunting for souvenirs. (Jem bought me a pair of silver hoop earrings). While touring in the jeepney, it rained so hard we could hardly see. I've never been on the top of a mountain in a heavy downpour, so it was quite an experience for me. After about twenty minutes the rain stopped and the sun came out again. While in the jeepney we passed a Hyatt Hotel with a sign saying that they had a casino and Gene let us know that he was anxious to risk his five dollars. We returned to our hotel, relaxed an hour or so and then ventured out to find a place to eat dinner. We ended up at the Hyatt, where Gene went straight to the casino. Fiawna was not allowed in the casino, so Cynthia and I wandered through the nice little hotel shops with Fiawna. All of a sudden, Butch caught up with us and said, "Come quickly; my father hit the jackpot!" We rushed up the escalator behind Butch and headed for the casino. Butch held Fiawna while Cynthia and I ran over to Gene. Gene had won 30,000 pesos ($1500). Immediately there was excitement all over the hotel; at least on the floor where the casino was located. Filipinos were coming out of the woodwork to look at the black American who hit the jackpot. Gene had come to Manila on a shoestring in the first place and no one was more deserving. We were all very, very excited. The managers of the casino crowded around the back and the side of Gene's machine, making all sort of adjustments. And Gene played the same one-arm bandit for a few more minutes and hit the jackpot again! He was so excited and afraid of being robbed by some suspicious looking Filipinos that he handed all those pesos to Butch, to hold. Gene then treated us to dinner in the Hyatt's most expensive restaurant. We had a grand time. It was the first time I tasted pickled papaya, and it was delectable. Gene. unwittingly gave the waiter a tip that was larger than the waiter's salary for a whole month. But Gene was feeling GOOD. As nice as the dinner was though, it did not compare to any of Cynthia's dinners. And I'm certain that none of us will ever forget the day

Gene broke the bank at Baguio.

Labor Day at 5 a.m. we were on the road, leaving Baguio. It was still dark out and we somehow took the wrong fork in the road after partially descending the mountain and ended up at the entrance of a mining field (silver mine). We also passed the famous Philippine Military Academy, the equivalent of our West Point. The sunrise accompanied us the rest of the way down the mountain and it was truly a sight to behold.

After descending the mountain and while on flat terrain, somewhere along the way we encountered army trucks parked alongside the main highway. The soldiers were out of the trucks and their backs were towards us. It turned out to be a pee stop.

We arrived home before noon and Cynthia treated us to a lovely informal lunch of a combination of chicken, tuna salad and crab meat and cheese, on toast, sprinkled with powdered sugar; a wooden bowl of watermelon chunks, a big glass mug of combined cherry or strawberry and lemon Koolaid, with a straw with a little decorative parasol stuck in a twisted orange slice and tipped to one side of the mug; all served on individual bamboo trays and brought to us wherever we were in the house at the time. It was almost too pretty to eat. In fact, I grabbed my camera but I got so excited that I used the wrong setting, which resulted in only a half shot of the tray.

After lunch, Cynthia put Fiawna in a stroller and took me on a tour of the neighborhood. We didn't stroll far. It was too hot.

Labor Day evening Cynthia and Butch took us to a jazz club in Olongapo, which featured a guitar, a bass, a keyboard, and drums. As soon as the leader saw us enter, the quartet began to play "Blue Monk." It seems that the fellows had gone there a prior evening and when they were handed a slip of paper on which to place their request, they had written "Blue Monk," but the group played "Blue Moon" instead. And upon noticing that the quartet had a fake music book, our guys did a little research and sure enough found "Blue Monk." So now the quartet was bursting with pride with the new additon to their repertoire. We ordered drinks and Butch ordered calamari and shrimps for all of us, and we munched through two "sets." By then we all realized how tired we were from the Baguio trip, so we called it a night and dragged ourselves home to bed.

On the day after Labor Day Cynthia took me to the Loot Locker, on base. I'm really not a shopper, but I had a ball that day. Just sorry that I wasn't farsighted enough to purchase small gifts for Christmas, gifts that wouldn't have taken up too much space in my luggage. Believe me, the prices were RIGHT.

The next day Cynthia and I had appointments at the hairdresser, on base, where all the beauticians were Filipinos. I was "Yes-mommed" and "No-mommed" to death, and received the royal treatment for only $3.85. Wash, dry and set. My hair turned out nicely, except that it was such a soft set that by the time we reached the house in all that heat, I had no curls. But at those prices, who could complain. One could go to the hairdresser twice a day if one had to. That night Cynthia had planned a completely Mexican dinner and it was scrumptious.

September 8th was a banner day. After breakfast we took a taxi to an office on base where I obtained ID (Jem and Gene already had theirs) so that I could come and go as I pleased off base through the Main Gate, without Butch or Cynthia. I was photographed and fingerprinted (one finger only), and the ID was good for the duration of my stay in the Philippines. As soon as I received my ID Jem and I walked through the Main Gate and mingled with the natives. A strange feeling went over me when I showed my pass at the Main Gate; and I realized I was a long way from home. We stopped at a sidewalk camera shop because we couldn't get the lens off Jem's camera. While the proprietor was working on the camera, the heat was so intense that I decided to sit in a cool, little alcove on the side of the camera stand. From where I sat I could see Jem and he could see me. But as people would pass by the alcove, they only saw me sitting there alone. Many people looked in my direction as they passed by, most of whom were Filipinos. A few black men passed by with Filipino girls and a few white men with Filipino girls. Then along came a white man alone. He looked in my direction as he passed by, did a double take, took a step back and came into the alcove and sat on the bench next to the bench where I was sitting. I kept looking straight ahead but could see Jem as well as the man sitting on the bench to my left. I do not believe that the man was within Jem's view. I saw the man turn his head in my direction. I never moved my head. The man looked away. After about five minutes of silence and non-motion on the part of the white man, Jem gave me the high sign and I stood up and walked to the sidewalk, where Jem joined me. The man, upon seeing Jem, looked perplexed. Jem and I walked away.

As we strolled down the street, heading for Toby, the American sandal maker, I heard a gunshot; then a siren. I grabbed Jem's hand and said, "Let's go back on the base." He hesitated but said, "No, let's just turn down this street." Meantime, a native male came up to us and said, "It's okay; just a fire drill." Jem and I looked at each other. We were standing near a combination fire house/police station.

We arrived at Toby's and a sketch was made of my feet. My sandals were ready the next day. The heat was so unbearable that we returned to the Main Gate and took a taxi back to the house. The taxis only operated on the base.

When everyone was home for dinner we heard that Gene had been Murph'd on Murphy Street. Mind you, this was after his big winnings in Baguio. He took a ride on a trike in Olongapo and ended up at somebody's house where he was duped for $40 after being forced to play cards. Gene, the ex-New York City slicker! When Gene escaped from that house and complained, agents arrived and asked Gene, "Do you want them iced?" I understand that if Gene had said yes, the culprits would have been killed on the spot.

One day at a bar owned by a black American, Jem beat Butch at two games of chess. At dinner that night Butch announced that he had invited someone over after dinner to play chess with Jem, since Jem was so hot. So after dinner, in walked Edmundo, Assistant to the Mayor of Olongapo, in charge of the power plant. Edmundo brought his chess set with him. Before Edmondo arrived, Jem and Gene were teasing Butch, saying that the guy that

Butch invited was probably a ringer. Well, Edmundo won the first game so fast it left Jem's head spinning. And before we realized it, Edmundo had won a second game. The rest of us were watching a movie on the VCR. And during the second game Jem had called out, "How's the movie?" I guess we all knew then that Jem was in trouble. Edmundo turned out to be a ringer sure enough. He is a tournament chess player, plays every day, and has world standing. Jem plays maybe twice a year. After the second game Cynthia brought out a homemade birthday cake with two candles; one for Butch and one for me. Butch's birthday was that day, but mine was the next week. Everyone toasted us with chmpagne, and gifts were brought out of hiding; for both of us. Butch received a very handsome ornamental pyramid, material for the seamstress to make him a suit, bright fabric for play clothes and some cashew nuts. And to my surprise, I received a necklace and earrings of terra-cotta, a card, and an elegant straw basket. Cynthia says that no one should go to the Philippines and not take home a basket.

Butch sat talking with Edmundo and Jem for quite a while. We could hardly wait for Edmundo to leave, so we could jump on Butch. We couldn't believe that Butch would do such a thing. As soon as the door was shut behind Edmundo, Jem, Gene, Cynthia and myself all started talking at the same time. Butch put up his hands and said "All right, all right, here's the real deal." And right in front of our eyes Butch became an Intelligence Agent. It seems that Butch needed some vital information that he could only get through Edmundo, and he needed the info by the next morning. And the only way Butch could do this, without raising suspicion with the mayor's office, was to invite Edmundo over to the house to play chess.

Saturday, September 10, was beach-party-birthday-celebration day and the whole household journeyed to the marina with a truck full of food; loaded ourselves and lots of Butch's Filipino friends, and all the food onto a boat for the 40-minute ride to Grande Island, a naval retreat but now opened to the public. Cynthia and Butch had the use of a kitchen and dining hall where Cynthia, with Lita's help, proceeded immediately to set up a banquet. Cynthia had brought tons of food and the Filipinos brought more. There were cheeses and crackers, potato chips, tortilla chips, dips, pickles, a whole roast pig, barbecue chicken, crabs, prawns, noodles, raw cauliflower, raw broccoli, fresh native fruits, fresh regular fruits, many different rice dishes, a salmon mold, jello molds of pineapple, coconut, nuts and marshmallows; watermelon, candy, punch, soda and beer. There was music, swimming, political discussions, business discussions, but most of the time was spent eating.

Nightfall found us back on the boat heading for home. Butch had given Gene the key to the house because the three of us would reach home before Cynthia and Butch. Since Gene is always misplacing things, Jem said, "Gene, give me the key. I'll put it in my shirt pocket, the pocket that doesn't have a hole in it." So Gene surrendered the key. The boat docked and we walked from the marina to the Main Gate and took a taxi to the house. The driver left after he was paid and we climbed the steps to the house. The house was dark inside but the outside lights were all lit. Jem fumbled in his pocket. All of a sudden he started cussing. He couldn't find the key. But he did find a hole in the pocket where he had placed the key. A new bathroom was being built in the master bedroom and the area was closed off with only plywood walls. Gene went to the back of the house and neatly busted through the wall and let us in through the front door. Jem was so embarrassed, to say the least.

Whenever I think of Grande Island I'll always think of Lita, the maid. This was the first time we saw her with makeup on and she was looking exceptionally pretty. The young Filipino fellows on the boat, as well as those on Grande Island who joined us there, were eyeing her and she was blushing and eyeing them back. One fellow worked with her in the kitchen the whole time. He was even interested in coming to the house to visit her. Lita had the biggest smile on her face all day, even when she was carrying Fiawna on one hip. Lita is 26 years old, and single.

The next day was the last day on the base for Jem and me. Butch had hoped to take us to Corregidor Island, but the cruise and tour were cancelled by the authorities. Cynthia made a terrific breakfast, after which Butch drove us to the area where the Negritos (black people of the Philippines) lived, right on the base.

The Negritos are said to be descendants of the first settlers of Manila. We did not go on their reservation but we saw one man walking along the road and a few others working at a nearby golf course. They were black like me, with kinky hair, like mine. They are the only people that were not displaced by the naval base. But seeing them and learning of their way of life truly reminded me of the struggle of the black race in the States.

Later, Butch and Gene drove us into Manila, to the Westin Plaza Hotel, right on Manila Bay. Gene was not returning to the States with us. We were to spend a couple of days at this hotel before returning to Frisco. During the drive on the Road of Life, Butch drove in his usual death-defying, crazy manner but this time some jerk on a trike on the side of the road held his arm out and we passed so close to him that his hand hit the car with such a bang that I'm sure he must have lost a finger or part of one anyway. We never stopped. There seems to be an unwritten rule that if a foreigner has an accident on the road, if you can help it, you never stop because the natives will surround you and you will always be the one at fault, and it may cost you a lot of money.

At one point when we were on the better road, closer to Manila than Olongapo, Butch tried to get a certain station on the car radio. He already knew that his antenna was broken but now he went into a tirade against all Filipinos. He was sure some Filipino had broken off his antenna, even though Butch didn't see anyone do it. He said, "You can't park your car in certain neighborhoods;" that they steal you blind, that they're shiftless and lazy; that they play loud music, that all they want to do is party, that they smell badly and they don't take baths. He had us cracking up with laughter because he sounded exactly like whitey talking about us.

The Plaza is considered the top hotel in Manila, and I could see why. It was not only beautiful but beautifully situated at the Bay. The view from our little balcony was unbelievable, like a great painting. I saw my first true Manila sunset, with ships in the harbor, and I managed to capture it with my camera.

This was actually my birthday and Jem took me to dinner at the most exclusive restaurant in the hotel. We dined to music by a live combo consisting of a guitar, two violins, a piano, a flute, and a male singer that sang so sensuously that I wanted to bring him home with me. This restaurant had odd foods like quail eggs, for appetizers, along with thinly sliced coconut and black olives; ordinary entrees fancily prepared, and desserts like mango pie and avocado souffle. The musicians became troubadours and wandered from table to table; all except the pianist of course. And when the troubadours took a break a different pianist came and played old American standards from a book; tunes like "Summertime," "Danny Boy" and "Clair de Lune." I was impressed and was vigorously applauding each number until she played "Way Down Upon The Swanee River." The troubadours soon returned and we finished our dessert. As we left the restaurant the maitre d' handed me a fresh, long-stemmed red rose.

The next day we took a tour of Manila, seeing several historic spots, including the palace where Imelda Marcos' shoes were on display. Except this was not a day when the palace was open to tourists, so we couldn't go inside. We also visited the largest military cemetery in the world, filled with people from all over the world who fought and died in World War II. It was a beautiful place with white, stone columns listing those buried there. Also there was a small chapel from which music flowed outside to the grounds. While we were there I heard "Amazing Grace" and "Come by Here, Lawd." We were driven through the wealthy Forbes area of Manila, all spacious, lush and green and clean; and then through the poor section with crowded, dirty streets and barefoot kids playing basketball, Manila's national sport.

As I thought about our return trip to the States, to Frisco to be exact, I suggested we upgrade our flight for those 16 long hours. So we made arrangements at our hotel to upgrade. It was suggested that we go in person to Philippine Airlines' Office to pay the difference in price. So after our tour we went to the office, which was near our hotel. We sat until our number was called. When we found out that upgrading would cost us $500 each, we flipped. Jem said, "Well, we'll keep our original reservations at tourist rates." When the clerk checked and came back to us she informed us that by making the upgraded reservation, our original reservation had been cancelled and had already been given to two other people. Jem jumped from his chair and shouted in my direction, "I TOLD YOU NOT TO FOOL AROUND WITH PHILIPPINE AIRLINES. NOW LOOK AT THE PREDICAMENT WE'RE IN. I TOLD YOU. MAYBE NEXT TIME YOU'LL LISTEN TO ME. WE'LL TAKE ANYTHING BUT PHILIPPINE AIRLINES. I TOLD YOU; I TOLD YOU.!" The clerk tried to calm Jem down. I had a hard time keeping a straight face, knowing that Jem was acting. Finally the clerk said, "Let me see what I can do." She walked away and Jem sat down and winked at me. The clerk returned and said, "Can you leave tomorrow, instead of your original day;" which would have been two days away. And Jem nearly screamed, "Yes!"

Now unbeknownst to Jem, when I arranged our vacation itinerary I had purposely picked September 14 for the return trip rather than September 13 (I always tell myself I'm not superstitious, mind you). So now we were to leave on the 13th. But I was cool. I never said a word about this until we arrived safely in Frisco. I never even mentioned that on September 12, sometime in the middle of the night, my deceased Uncle PJ had peeked at me around a wall in our room. It must have been a dream.

Our flight back was without incident. In fact, when we landed in Honolulu where we had to deplane for an hour for the cleaning of the plane and a change of flight crew, the new crew turned out to be our original flight crew of two weeks prior. It was like being with old friends.

Upon landing in Frisco, we made our way to Vallejo and Toy picked us up at the bus depot. I do believe that we were as glad to see her as she was to see us. She had been alone for the first time in her many years of marriage to Gene. Previously, one of the children would have been home. She said she was just beginning to talk to herself. And we were just thrilled to be back in the States. Toy was still working, so Jem and I kept house for a couple of days-- he tinkering with the cars and me making dinner for a change. No maid service here. Jem took us to the movies one evening and to dinner another. And before we were rid of our jet lag it was time to head for our week in Daytona Beach, Florida.

We arrived in Daytona on a Saturday morning, rented a Cadillac (red was the only color available) and drove to the time-shared condo that had been loaned to us by friends who were traveling in the Far East. At last we were on Eastern Standard Time, and after a day or so we were back to normal as far as our built-in clocks were concerned. Having the car was great, but it proved to be too much for some Floridians. One evening, on our way into one of the famous Morrison Family Restaurants with a couple who had just relocated in Daytona Beach from St. Albans, New York; as we were alighting from our red Cadillac, a white man with a peculiar expression stood waiting for us to close our doors before he walked up to a car parked alongside ours. We went inside Morrison's and had a delightful meal. But when we came out, someone had taken a sharp object and scraped the paint for the whole length of our car, on the passenger side. The car had been in tip-top shape when we received it from Avis. Of course we don't know who did it, but we each had our suspicion.

The rest of our week in Florida was very relaxing. Jem let me drag him out at 7 a.m. a couple of mornings to try capturing Daytona sunrises; he with the Videocam and me with my Nikon. He thought himself crazy for being up and out at that hour, on vacation, but he was just as proud of his shots as I was of mine.

One day I contacted a guy who used to work with me, who is now retired and lives in Palm Coast, Florida, a forty-minute drive from where we were, and he and his wife invited us to stop by. When we pulled up into their driveway they ran out and hugged and kissed both of us as if we were long lost friends. Irene and George are white, and I wondered what their neighbors were thinking if any of them had witnessed the greeting. It was a real hot day and the lovebugs were all over the place. Lovebugs are odd-looking, fuzzy, black bugs that fly stuck to each other; flying into people, into things; a real nuisance. We immediately went indoors, which was, thank God, air-conditioned. Jem and George remembered each other from the job and it was funny to hear the three of us, all talking at once about different people and the changes on the job since George left. We were served ham sandwiches on rye, coffee made in George's old coffee pot that he used at work, and chocolate fudge cake which Irene had made, which was so delicious it was sinful to eat. They gave us the grand tour of their cozy, cheerfully decorated home. After spending a good two hours with them, it was easy to understand their greeting. They were starved for company. They had relocated from Nassau County, New York and George, an ex-POW, thrives on the peace and quiet of Palm Coast. Irene hates it. The only way we were able to get away from them was to promise to try and come back later in the week and stay longer. We got away, but we never returned. We did call them though.

One day we drove to Silver Spring Shores in Ocala, Florida, to surprise one of Jem's friends, but we got the surprise because they weren't home. Nevertheless, it was an interesting trip.

We visited Bethune/Cookman College, located right in the heart of Daytona Beach, and sat in on an actual rehearsal of their traveling chorus. Jem took video shots and I smuggled in my cassette-corder and taped the rehearsal. The results were fantastic.

On our last night in Daytona Beach we followed a carload of New Yorkers, who were vacationing at the same condo as we, to Coco Beach to listen to some live jazz. It was quite a long trip but a great way to end our vacation. I got goose pimples when I saw the road signs for Cape Canaveral.

Next afternoon, while awaiting clearance to land at La Guardia Airport our plane circled the area for a good ten minutes. It was one of those days where you could see forever and the view of Manhattan was one of the most beautiful that either of us had ever seen. And as luck would have it, the videocam was in the storage area above our seats. We were seated three abreast but neither of us was on the aisle. Instructions for landing had already been given and complied with. But had either of us been on the aisle we would have removed our seat belt and reached for the videocam. The man on the aisle, seated next to me, must not have been a photography buff because he said, "I'm afraid I can't get up now," after I asked if he would please reach the videocam so we could capture the magnificent scenes. And what would have been the greatest photo shots of our Adventure of the Summer of '88, and right in our own backyard so to speak, is now only a fading picture in our minds.

* * *

THIRD WORLD

My lifelong friend, Mary, had just dropped us off at Kennedy Airport, and we were on our way to Africa. A tall, slender, beautiful black girl sauntered up to Jem and, in broken English, asked where he was bound for and how much luggage he had. A short time later I had a similar experience with a young man. Each time, when the individual was told that our destination was Dakar, Senegal, they wanted to know could we do them a favor and check one of their bags with our luggage. Remembering all the narcotic cases in court where people are caught carrying luggage for someone else and not always knowing what's inside, be it narcotics or other contraband, we both quickly declined to "do them a favor." When we reached our check-in point and told our tour director of this strange encounter, she explained that this is the norm when you travel to Third World countries; that the people carry so many things back to their country that they always exceed the maximum pieces of luggage as well as the weight; and that sometimes strangers "do them a favor."

We had been given the name and a limited description of a fellow from Westchester County, New York, who frequents Dakar and who was in fact booked on our flight. His name was Ray, and the description was, "He's very tall." So upon our arrival at the gate at Kennedy, every time we saw a tall man one of us would go over and say, "Are you Ray?" No luck.

Our flight from Kennedy via Air Afrique, which is really a stepchild of Air France, was exceptionally smooth. Nearly all of the passengers were black; also the entire crew, including the pilot. When we were about five hours into our seven-hour flight, a tall man walked past our seat and I said to Jem, "I'll bet that was Ray." And before I could get another word out, an even taller man was about to pass by when I said, "Are you Ray?" And he said, "Yes; you must be Ellie and Jem." He inquired as to where we would be staying and said he and his wife, who was sitting way up front, would be in touch with us.

We landed late at night in this eighty percent Muslim country, and the heat was overbearing as we walked from the landing field into the airport. We entered to a mob scene and a few circulating high ceiling fans. Thankfully, our processing through customs didn't take too long.

The girls in our group of seven were not aware that they were part of a harem until we were about to board our tour van at the airport for the ride to our hotel. Because we were swarmed by peddlers, we were having a lot of difficulty climbing into the van. All of a sudden we heard, "ALL RIGHT, STAND BACK. THESE LADIES BELONG TO ME. STAND BACK EVERYBODY." Good old Jem to the rescue! There was Minnie, a retired school teacher; Judy, a cultural consultant (our tour director); Loris, an economics teacher; Cathy, a policewoman; Burlette, an attorney; and Jem, our senior member, and myself. Jem dubbed me Wife #1 and Judy was Wife #2, and so on. Except that Judy kept losing her spot whenever she did something that Jem disapproved of and somewhere along the trip she became #6. Also later in the trip Jem was told that the other "wives" were rebelling because they wanted equal time. That's the only occasion on the entire trip that Jem became speechless.

The twenty-minute ride to our hotel was uneventful, except that our driver went through a red light and crossed a railroad track where we saw the bright headlight of a train. When we complained, Alpha, the tour guide, smiled and said that they (he and the driver) could see there was no other traffic and they knew the train was standing still. I thought to myself, yeah, this might be your country, but it's our lives. And then I said a little prayer. Soon the landscape turned from a flat countryside full of road signs in French to tall, city buildings and then we were at our hotel. And it was air-conditioned.

Next morning we turned on the radio in our room and were amazed to hear the music of jazzman Thelonius Monk. The "radio" turned out to be a musak system that played a variety of music. It was quite a delight to hear the Christmas portion of Handel's Messiah in Africa in the middle of August, 1989. We tried to locate the person in charge of the musical selections to express our surprise and appreciation of their choice of music, but with our English and their French, we didn't get very far. Yes, all those blacks speaking fluent French really blew my mind. Whatever bad influences France left on Senegal, it sure left it with a beautiful language.

Before partaking in our buffet-style breakfast, we changed our American money into what was called CFA francs. The exchange was 240 CFA's for one U.S. dollar. We were positively rich!

We had been warned not to drink the water, so it was perfect when, at breakfast, we ordered water and the waiter brought a bottle of water imported from France; the cost of which was added to our bill. And after each meal if we didn't finish the bottle we merely took it with us.

Our first group outing was to Goree Island via a ferry ride from Dakar--Goree Island, where slaves were processed before being sent all over the world, including the United States; where hundreds of slaves at a time were housed in a two story stone building in cramped, low-ceiling cells; where family members were separated from each other; where spirits were broken until a slave attained the "right attitude" before being shipped off to a foreign country; where all the young females were housed together and given preferential treatment so they could be used for you-know-what. We saw a small cut in a wall forming the rough shape of a door on the back side of the building, which was on the water, where, when a slave went through that opening, that was the point of no return. They went directly onto a ship headed for far away lands. Eighty percent of the slaves shipped to our country came through Goree Island. It was a weird feeling indeed to be standing in this structure or in the little courtyard, listening to the lectures given by various tour guides to various groups of people and wondering if any of your direct ancestors had come this route or even putting yourself in the place of the people we were hearing about. It was a very emotional moment which brought tears and anger to some in our group. And some of the anger was vented immediately by one person in our group on a cluster of white French tourists taking the tour right behind us. It was a very strange reaction.

On the other side of Goree Island was a round building that looked like a fortress. We later learned that this was the filming location for the movie The Guns of Navarrone.

Today there are people residing on Goree Island. They are either very rich or very poor. Some are black; some are white. It was here that I saw my first half-naked little black child, in Africa, that is. There were many children. And if one child was given something, it was immediately shared with all the other children.

During our return trip on the ferry to Dakar, a striking young black girl handed me a book showing woven hair styles and suggested that I look through it; that she could weave my hair for a good price, in whatever style I chose. She said that she had gone to school to learn her trade; that she knew what she was doing, and that she was good at it.

It was my second day in Africa. I had a perm in my hair. The weather was very hot and I thought, yeah, why not get a weave job. Especially when she said it would last about four weeks and that I could shampoo it as often as I liked without the weave coming undone. She and Jem haggled over the price until the price was right, and we arranged that she would come to my hotel room about twenty minutes after the boat docked. The job was to take about two hours.

After she worked on my hair for about a half hour, who should drop by but Ray (from the plane) and his wife Cathy (referred to hereafter, where necessary, as Cathy S.) I now meet Ray's wife for the first time, and she's wearing braids; came from the States with them. Jem and Ray went down to the bar and Cathy S. stayed with me. She gave me moral support and made suggestions as the girl proceeded, modifying the style I had chosen. In an hour and forty five minutes the job was completed. Cathy S. thought I looked ten years younger, although she had never seen me with my old hair style (unless she saw me at the airport, unbeknowing to me). I looked in the mirror and went into shock. But Cathy S. convinced me to leave the weave in and suggested we go downstairs and hear what the boys would have to say.

My hair was woven close to the head, from the sides towards the back, with a circle design in the middle of the back. There was a part on the top right and the hair was combed to the left side and woven into braids, with extensions, so that the braids fell over my left eye. I felt rediculous, but I accompanied Cathy S. to the bar. Jem took one look and said, "Awright!" And when the girls in our tour group said they liked it, and Cathy S. said, "Ellie, she's good and she's fast," and Cathy S. wanted to have her hair redone by my girl-- I decided to keep my weave job; at least for the duration of our stay in Africa. This turned out to be a smart move because it lasted for more than four weeks. And the top would have lasted even longer had I not tired of it and returned to my old hairdo. When Jem saw that I had gotten rid of the weave job he yelled, "What happened to my African Princess??!"

After the approval of my new hairdo, the same evening Ray and Cathy invited us to dinner at an African family's home. They knew the family well and had eaten there many times. When I suggested that Ray call ahead to see if it was okay for them to bring us along, he said, "Sure. This is Africa. They always have plenty of food for everyone." (My mind immediately conjured up TV news in the States showing all the starving people in Africa). "Besides," Ray continued, "I already told them that you two are our 'tant' and 'oncle,' so it's perfectly all right."

Off we went with Ray and Cathy. They always share a fellow's apartment when they're in Dakar, a fellow by the name of Demba. And we were headed for Demba's family's home. We walked from our hotel, passed where Ray and Cathy stayed, and walked and walked and walked; all the while with fellows calling hello to Ray, and all the while hassled by peddlers. We finally arrived at a large, stone, corner house with many steps. At the first landing we entered a yard and we were introduced to a smiling lady who greeted us loudly and enthusiastically. We went up more steps and met a young lady beautifully dressed in Muslim fashion, in light blue silk, holding a newborn baby. We were introduced as tant and oncle. She smiled and greeted us softly but warmly. She was the lady of the house. The first lady we met was the maid. We were ushered into a living room which contained a large floor fan that was not working, a television, a VCR, and a large square table surrounded by couches on three sides. A little boy entered the room and came to each of us and shook our hand. Ray played with the little boy. It was obvious that they were buddies.

Shortly after our arrival we could smell food being prepared. But before we were served, the man of the house arrived from work and sat and talked with us. His wife never joined us. Soon the maid entered with a bowl of water and a towel. We washed our hands. She next brought in a basket of sliced French bread, followed by a huge platter of food which she sat in the center of the table and left the room. We sat in our seats but moved closer around the table. The outer circle of the tray had delicious tiny French fried potatoes. The next circle had chunks of tender grilled lamb. The innermost circle contained cooked onions. There were no plates and no eating utensils. You took a piece of bread, broke it and picked up a piece of lamb with the bread and ate it. You broke another piece of bread and sort of sopped up some onions and put it right into your mouth. You took a few of the potatoes right in your hand. The maid did bring forks later, but we didn't use them. It was a most delectable meal. I couldn't detect the seasoning on the onions, but they were luscious. For dessert, a large platter of fresh fruit was placed on the table; whole bananas, sliced mangoes and sliced papaya. There was only water to drink, and it was not bottled water. But Ray and Cathy assured us that they had never had a problem, so we took a chance. It was a delightful evening, and the water gave us no problem.

On our way back home the four of us got into a taxi, which broke down after going only two blocks. About a dozen youths came out of nowhere and pushed the taxi to the side of the road. It was a scarry moment but I soon realized they were just being helpful. Our driver, who seemed very embarrassed, tried to start the car again but we thanked him and got out and took another taxi.

The following day we were taken on a city tour, which included a demonstration of the art of sand painting, and shopping in a tourist trap run by the government, where the peddlers reverently greeted Jem with, "Hello, my father." We saw many deformed people, young and old, begging in the open market area; some with fingers or toes missing. One young deformed girl slid along in the dirt, on her bottom, reaching out with one hand while balancing herself on the ground with the other. When we returned to our tour van and sat waiting for the rest of the group, we noticed several native little boys come over to the young girl and hand her something and she gave them something in return and they went on their way. It turned out they were working (begging) for her, for a price. We also saw the colorful open flower market, the cultural sites, the President's palace with the statuesque guard dressed in a red uniform; the street peddlers with their carts of peanuts, black walnuts, mangoes, tiny tomatoes and miniature bananas; and the mighty Boaboa tree, every part of which is good for some useful purpose, medicinal or otherwise. We even saw a Sharp brand "boom box." And in a supermarket we noticed TV's and VCR's for sale.

On our second day in Dakar we were introduced to a handsome, slight -of- build, extremely black young fellow with the whitest teeth and the prettiest smile. His name was Mamadou (Ma -ma-doo). He could get you anything you wanted, for a price of course. He would even accompany you whenever you left your hotel and take you, by taxi, wherever you wanted to go. He made you feel so comfortable, like he was a close friend or a family member. And he was always available. One young lady in our group really took to him, or they took to each other. And Mamadou was always hanging around. One day he invited us to his mother's village for lunch, a great distance from our hotel; but only Judy and Burlette opted to go. The same day Minnie and I were taken to an SOS Children's Village right in Dakar by a female Mamadou (That's what Jem dubbed the "professional" hustlers.) We met the director and the office staff and we were given a tour of the Village; met some of the children and a house mother who was taking care of the newest arrivals to the Village (twins from Muritania). Just as we were leaving it began to rain, torrents of rain; even though when we arrived for our short visit the sun was shining and the sky was blue. But our taxi did a yoeman's job in returning us safely to our hotel because in no time at all the streets were flooded and Dakar was a sea of potholes filled with muddy water. It was then I heard that there is no drainage system in all of Dakar.

Usually our group met for dinner each day, right in our hotel. When we went to dinner this day we learned that Burlette and Judy hadn't been heard from since they had left early afternoon with Mamadou, heading for his mother's village. When we realized that we didn't know where they had gone or how to reach them, and that we didn't even know Mamadou's full name, Minnie began to panic. The rest of us reasoned that they were probably stuck in a flooded area with no phone or no way to notify us. Just when Minnie was about to go off the deep end, the girls showed up with Mamadou. And our reasoning had been on the mark. Minnie did not eat her dinner that night, but when she got herself together we were a happy group of seven again.

One afternoon Jem and I walked over to the hotel where Jem had stayed on his previous trip to Dakar. In the lobby was this big, black, tall man with a large gold chain and a medallion around his neck. He spoke to us. His name was Mamadou. And he was with a group of tourists that was staying at our hotel. I began to wonder if all professional hustlers were called Mamadou or whether this was just a coincidence.

One day we hired two taxicabs to take the seven of us, plus "our" Mamadou into the countryside. We visited the equivalent of a slaughter house where hundreds of people were gathered in the open with their goats and cows. Our driver said it was okay to get out of the car and take pictures. We did. But the flies and the looks on the faces of some of the people drove me back into the car in no time. Most of the men looked like shepherds of old, wearing long garments, wide hats and carrying a staff. Our next stop was at the "Palm Beach Hotel," where we sat on the beach amid the stares of all the white people. We visited Lac Rose (Pink Lake) where the lake actually looks pink and from which lake white salt is processed. We tried to take pictures at the lake but the workers demanded money or something in exchange. I took one photo in exchange for a pencil. From there we went to a monastery tucked way back in a quiet section of a tiny village. The chapel was beautifully decorated in black, white and red murals, even on the ceiling, and in one area there were displayed instruments from biblical times. The priests sold us perfume and blank greeting cards, also of black, white and red designs, but with no envelopes.

The setting was so quiet and peaceful that all you could hear outside was the singing of birds.

Ray invited our group to a disco called Sahel, owned by his friend Demba, but not everyone was interested. Demba called for Jem and me at our hotel and drove us, in his Mercedes, to Sahel.

It was a fine disco, spacious and pretty. When we arrived Loris and Cathy R. were already disco-ing away under the strobe lights, each one dancing alone. As the evening wore on, once in a while a fellow would dance with one or the other, or maybe two fellows would join them. But basically they danced solo. And Cathy R. was a machine that never stopped. The music was good, with a nice beat. We danced a little, but mostly spent the evening talking with Ray, Cathy S. and Demba; and watching Loris and Cathy R. From that evening on Loris and Cathy R. went dancing each night, into the wee hours, but at different discos. They were late for breakfast every morning and always showed up half asleep. They would tell us some of the dialogue from the night before where the African fellows would "hit" on them, saying "I love you; I want to marry you." And Loris or Cathy would say, "Yeah, sure. You just want to get to America." And then Loris would get angry and accuse the Africans of "ripping off" all the tourists. And the fellows would retort, "Sure, we rip you off. But at least we don't do it with guns, like they do in your country." Loris and Cathy R. are the ones who should be writing this travel paper, not I. The musical entertainer at dinner in our hotel composed a song for Loris one evening, right on the spot, and sung it for us. The men were struck by her looks.

After one week in Dakar our van started out for The Gambia, a small English-speaking country about six hours driving time from Dakar. It had been raining for two days and our tour guide said we could start out but he didn't know if we could make it because a lot of the roads were washed out. It seemed as if we drove through rivers before reaching the main highway but we finally outdrove the rain, reached a dry road and found ourselves under blue skies. We drove through many villages with thatched huts, dogs, goats, cows, some five-feet-high ant hills, a monkey in the thick bush here and there, and roadside stands of roasted corn on the cob, mangoes and nuts. We saw several dogs throughout our travels in both countries and never heard one bark. Most of the villages looked as if they were frozen in time from the days when Jesus walked the earth; men with long frocks and women carrying pottery on their heads. We had to stop at a checkpoint just before the border and immediately our van was surrounded with reaching hands. They were the hands of children, begging for everything, in their native tongue. One child pointed to whatever she could see on me from outside the window of our van and motioned that I should give it to her. She was very cunning and was dressed much nicer and neater than all the other children. I'd like to call her a city slicker. She pointed to my rain hat, my sunglasses, my watch, my ring, my earrings. She pointed to her lips, asking for lipstick and to her fingernails, asking for fingernail polish. And each time, I shook my head no. Then she pointed to my pocketbook and I shook my head definitely no. She persisted, seeming to point to a specific area of my pocketbook. My eyes followed to where she was pointing and I suddenly realized she was indicating a rose colored pencil that was sticking up from the outer pocket of my pocketbook. I didn't dare give it to her while our van was sitting still because there were so many children and I had only one pencil with me at the time. I motioned to the child to just wait there. And just before our van pulled off, I quickly handed the pencil to her. She looked as if to say, "I knew I could make her give me something!" At this point I was struck at the sight of the face of another young girl. It was the face of a co-worker back in the States, except this face in Africa was black. I told myself right then and there that I would make up a bag of goodies for this young girl with the hope that she would be at that same spot when we returned.

We crossed the border and drove a short distance to a ferry that would take us to Banjul, The Gambia. While waiting to enter upon the ferry we were assailed by money changers as well as peddlers. And when we did board the ferry it was crowded with trucks and vans and cars and lots of people, the majority of whom seemed to be peddlers. At first, we got out of the van to stretch our legs and to inhale the fresh air. Five minutes later most of us reentered the van, trying to escape the peddlers. We had to close the windows for fear the hands would reach inside forever offering bargains. We were trapped in the van with no fresh air for nearly the entire 45-minute ride. When we docked we drove through streets of red mud, crowded with people. My heart went out to everyone on foot, especially to the beautifully dressed native women trying to make their way through the mud. Our hotel was some distance from the heart of town and as we rode along someone commented on the strange color of most of the cars. We soon figured out that the cars were covered with the red mud. When finally we turned off the muddy highway we went through a neat green village and ended up at paradise. We were at our hotel.

One building housed the front desk, a comfortable lobby with couches and tables and gorgeous flowers, a gift shop, a bar, a disco, a dining room, a poolside restaurant and a snack bar. The other building housed the guest rooms. And in between the two buildings there was a walkway landscaped with palm trees, colorful flowers, a huge Boaboa tree, a giant-sized black and white chess set where each piece stood on a giant black and white checkered floor, and an inviting swimming pool. Behind all this was a beach and the Atlantic Ocean.

The currency in The Gambia is called Dalasi and we only received 7.27 Dalasi for one American dollar, so we lost our wealthy status. But there was a plus-- everyone spoke English. Oh, there was a native dialect, but almost everyone spoke English.

On our first evening in The Gambia we had drinks at poolside with several officials of Gambia; someone from the Police Department, someone from the courts, someone from the parliament and several others in high places; all arranged by Judy. It was an interesting session.

The food in The Gambia was very good and there was much more of a variety, a welcomed change from the rice and fish or rice and chicken that we ate in Dakar.

One evening Judy was instrumental in getting all of us to meet at the disco. And some of the fellows we had met that first night met us there. At one point Jem, who is a great dancer, was on the dance floor dancing with all of us. Before we knew it everyone else was pointing to Jem and commenting, "That's the guy with all the wives." But that didn't stop some of the "wives" from later pairing off with the young fellows. It was a fun night.

Whenever we went shopping in The Gambia the peddlers who had stalls would step outside and say, "We're family. Come into my shop and bring me luck. I have a good buy for you." They'd act insulted if you didn't enter their shop. And if you did go into their shop and failed to purchase anything, they really got upset.

Burlette, Jem and I went to a tiny country Methodist church on Sunday morning. There was no choir and the piano was broken; couldn't be used at all. A man sat next to the piano and whenever a hymn was about to be sung he would stand up and lead the congregation into the song. After each stanza there was somewhat of a pause and then he would continue and everyone followed. It was done like clockwork, and the timing was fascinating to me. The harmonizing was such that I have never heard bcforc, very pleasing to the ear. The sermon was based on mutual respect in marriage and the pastor said that he had been asked that the church pray for a Muslim woman whose husband had left her and the children for three months, supposedly seeking employment, and she hadn't heard from him and knew nothing of his whereabouts. We were welcomed as visitors by the minister from the pulpit but the small congregation did not welcome us as warmly as I had thought they would. One face had stood out when I was in church, the face of a very black, well-dressed woman with a proud African profile.

After church we joined the others back at the hotel, changed into casual clothes and went to the home of an assistant representative of UNICEF (United Nations Children's Fund) where we had been invited for lunch. Sitting in her living room made me feel that I was in a Greenwich Village townhouse that had just had a decorating job. I couldn't believe I was in Africa. It turned out to be an international luncheon, with most of the people being connected with UNICEF and each person bringing their favorite dish or cooking it after they arrived. We met an administration finance assistant of UNICEF, someone from the Ministry of Education, UNICEF World Food Programme School Garden

Project, from England; a Fisheries Department Assistant, from Italy; an assistant representative of UNICEF, from Korea; a journalist from Virginia, working at the Center For Foreign Journalists; an Italian man working with the Department of Highways (and did we get on him about all the mud); and a lady from the House of Parliament in Banjul, The Gambia.

The food was artfully prepared and most delicious. Our hostess even made a birthday cake for Judy, whose birthday was the following week. And after lots of eating, drinking and talking, trying to get to know one another, some very loud recorded music was played in a room away from where we were, music with a Latin/Turkish/Moroccan beat. A strip of bright colored fabric, each different from the other, was given to each of us, which we were told to tie around our hips. Everyone danced and danced and danced. Jem made a great videotape of this scene and it makes me laugh each time I look at it. We had such a good time, especially when Cathy R. ended up dancing with Stephen, from Rome, whom she couldn't stand. All too soon it was time for us to go home and change clothes and keep our appointment with the Honorable Mrs. Louis N'Jie, Minister of Health, Labour and Social Welfare (affectionately called "Auntie Lou.") She turned out to be the lady I noticed in church with the proud African profile. She was very warm and gracious, receiving us in her own home. And I am left with a very favorable, lasting impression.

The day after the party we visited the director of community development and then took a field trip to the UNICEF School Garden Project in a village called Pirang. Before we left the States it had been suggested that we might want to make a presentation to the children at this school. And we had brought along our gifts.

When we arrived we were met by Anne from England, whom we had met at the party; the most unlikely looking person that you would expect to see on a motorcycle. But there she was. We observed the garden under a hot sun and bright blue sky. Then we entered into a one-room school with crude wooden benches and tables and a dirt floor, a tin roof and an open upper wall with a roof overhang that served as a window. The director of the school spoke to us through an interpreter. Then the top student in the garden project spoke to us, also through an interpreter. The director had mentioned that the children needed supplies to work with but that there was no money for the purchase of anything. And then Minnie, our retired teacher, along with Loris, made the presentation to the little boy of the things we had brought for them; pencils, paper, crayons, chalk, erasers, construction paper, scissors, et cetera. The director and the child were near tears of thanks when we heard a loud noise that startled us. It was the sudden, heavy downpour of rain hitting the tin roof of the school. Jem said it was as if God Himself was saying thank-you to us.

One day in The Gambia everyone went into town to shop and I stayed behind and walked the beach with my camera. I met an English lady who had been teaching for a month in an African village and she was now on her way back to Canada. Together we watched the fishermen pull in a net full of fish, and I got one shot that looks like a picture postcard. She left me on the beach to go pack her things. And after watching young people playing ball on the beach and trying not to stare at an interracial couple strolling along while I sneaked pictures of ladies in bright colors carrying baskets on their heads, I headed back to my room. As I left the beach and came to the pool, just ahead of me was a shapely, young white female who was topless. I asked her could I take her picture. She said, "My picture?" I said, "Yes." She asked, "Why would you want my picture?" I replied, "Are you kidding? No one in New York will believe me when I tell them about you." She retorted, in her thick British accent, "Oh, everyone in New York goes around like this;" to which I responded, "Believe me, they don't!" So she threw out her arms and pulled up her rib cage and said, "Okay, shoot." Thereafter, whenever she saw me she would give me a vigorous wave.

Sure enough, on our return to Dakar when we stopped at the border there was the little girl with the familiar face. When our van stopped I caught her eye and beckoned her to come to my window. When she did, I handed her the "bag" I had put together for her. It contained pencils, paper, crayon, two sun hats, fingernail polish, lipstick, perfume, candy and tissues. She pointed to herself as if to say, "For me?" And I nodded my head "Yes." Her eyes grew big and sparkled like the sun reflecting on a pool of clear water. She took the bag and ran to a woman nicely dressed in Muslim fashion, who I presumed to be her mother, and pushed the bag into the woman's hand. The lady looked down in the bag and said something to the child. The child pointed to me sitting in the van. The lady looked in my direction; bowed and smiled as if I had given them a million bucks in American money. That moment was the highlight of my trip to Africa.

It's hard to believe, but whatever we throw away here in the USA the Africans, especially those in back villages, can use; from food scraps to old shoes, old jewelry, old clothes, pieces of pencils, pieces of paper, a paper bag, a plastic bag, an old hat, a cardboard box, a tiny piece of soap and on and on and on. The children beg for pencils and our children here in the USA don't bother to go to school.

The scene at the airport in Dakar at 2 a.m. was bedlam and the temperature was very warm. Our tour guide had done the best he could to get us as close to the locked gates which would eventually allow us entry into the main airport area. And we were jammed in like cattle, with no one giving us any information. All we could do was stand where we were. What seemed like hours later the main gates were opened and then came the pushing to check the luggage. Hours later we were told our plane would be coming in at a particular location. We went to that location, only to be told no, it will come in "over there." We went "over there," only to be told to go back where we came from. When the plane did arrive there were passengers on board, so there were no reserved seats for anyone boarding in Dakar. We had to run for seats. And if you didn't get a seat, you couldn't fly; and planes leave Dakar for the States only twice a week. So picture this: We walked out of the airport onto the field, with our luggage, cameras and presents, et cetera, and hiked, half-running, what seemed like a half a mile to the steps of the plane and then had to engage in a pushing session in order to go up the ladder of steps to actually enter the plane. Jem was way ahead of me, carrying the heavier things, and a guy behind me was acting like I wasn't even there. Jem said later that he heard a mousy voice say, "All right, you want to push?! I'll show you how to push!" It was my voice. I was just pretending I was on a crowded subway train in New York. And although a stewardess scolded the man in French, who was pushing me, he only stopped momentarily. When I reached the top of the steps, about to enter the plane, there he was, trying to go over me again. But Jem had gotten two seats and I sat down and tried to catch my breath. I felt like a lowly animal that had just survived a stampede. I was not ready for this. My trip was ruined. And it will be quite some time before I'm ready to visit another Third World country.

* * *

THE FRIENDS

We pulled up to the parking attendant at 6:55 p.m. on Saturday, June 2, 1990 and presented our personal parking pass, forwarded to us by our hostess; parked the car, picked up our video camera, the Nikon and the Ricoh, and boarded the yacht along with an international group of beautiful people. Jem and I wore blue blazers, white slacks, white shoes and white captain's hats. We pretended we owned the yacht.

As we boarded, we were handed a wine glass of dark bubbly, which was quite tasty. We mingled, sipping wine, our glasses being refilled with champagne by the waiters. The mother of the bride was stunning in her pale pink two-piece, beaded dress.

A half hour later, music could be heard from the speakers and the Maid of Honor slowly walked into the main deck, closely followed by the bride. The gown was a long, white, strapless, beaded dress with a long, silk taffeta train. The bride's hair was combed back into one braid, with a large white taffeta bow.

A most lovely bride, the product of a mixed marriage (German mother; black father). She speaks English, German and French. The groom is of Jewish descent, from Switzerland. The two met as children years ago when the bride spent her childhood summers sometimes in Switzerland and sometimes in Germany. So they grew up as friends. All grown up now, she in law school here in New York and he, working in banking (foreign exchange) in Switzerland, was transferred to New York.

The ceremony was performed by a female ecumenical minister, who was very animated and knew her craft well. It was a simple, warm and touching ceremony, with both parties avowing their own pledge to each other. They were the happiest looking bride and groom I have ever seen.

Immediately after the ceremony the minister went ashore and we set sail up the Hudson. A table of appetizers was then set up consisting of fancy cold noodles shaped like shrimp, raw vegetable salad, pate, cole slaw, French bread, chopped liver and Roquefort cheese balls. At the same time the waiters were serving hors d'oeuvres of fried ravioli, boneless chicken on a stick, fried Brie cheese balls, and lox on brown bread squares.

After everyone had kissed the bride and congratulated the groom, we were invited to the lower deck for a sit-down dinner consisting of a salad, a choice of filet mignon or poached salmon, served with wild rice and mixed steamed vegetables of cauliflower, brocolli and carrots. I chose the salmon, which melted in my mouth.

Next to each dinner plate was a tiny, white, shiny box, the top of which was indented into the shape of a flower. A label on the side of the box read, "Truffler - A collection of fine Swiss chocolates." The box was tied with a narrow, dusty rose ribbon. Attached to the ribbon were two miniature pink, silk roses with a silk spray of green, with dusty rose silk leaves. And inside each box was one piece of chocolate candy.

On the lower deck there was live music and a DeeJay; also a small dancing area, which was almost always crowded. And the bride did her share of lindy-hopping and the twist, even though she still wore her gown.

The table of desserts was sinful. There was mixed fresh fruits, Mississippi Mud Cake (thick chocolate fudge with nuts), five layer chocolate cake, cheese cake, ice cream, coffee and tea. The wedding cake was filled with chocolate pudding.

Before we reached the George Washington Bridge the yacht turned around and headed south; entered into the East River, passed South Street Seaport, went under the Brooklyn Bridge, the Manhattan Bridge, the Williamsburg Bridge, turned around again and headed back towards the Battery, passed close by the Statue of Liberty and headed up the Hudson once more. Each time we looked out the windows there was another spectacular view of Manhattan after dark.

The wedding invitation read:

"Today, I will marry my friend.

Please share this special day with us on
Saturday, the second of June
Nineteen hundred and ninety
at seven o'clock in the evening (sharp)
on the 'Riveranda'
of the
World Yacht Cruise Pier 62
West 23rd Street Hudson River New York, New York

Monique Jackson *Rene Meyer"*

We docked at 11:30 p.m. with an invitation to dance the night away at a club called Stringfellow's on East 21st Street.

* * *

AND THEY WAVED US GOOD-BYE

His Eye Is On The Sparrow, as only Mahalia Jackson could sing it, was floating from one of the three reel-to-reel tapes on the wall. It was Thanksgiving Day in the States. But here we were seated at a table in an exclusive, private supper club in Tokyo about to be served dinner. Stan spoke out: "I sure wish they wouldn't play that song right now; I really don't want to hear it. It reminds me of my mother." I looked across the table at Etta, whose eyes were staring as if she were miles away, and I knew she was thinking of her daughter Kathy, who died a few years ago. Jem was staring into space and I knew he was thinking of his sister Lucille, who passed in August. And Houston commented that this would be his children's first Thanksgiving without their mother, who had died recently. Yes, Thanksgiving Day. And we were all so very far from home. I wanted to reach out to each one of them and give them a big hug all at the same time, but I couldn't. I searched my brain for something fitting to say, but nothing came, so I kept quiet. It was a sad few moments. I thought the song would never end.

The beautiful, fashionable, young Japanese hostesses, looking like they had just stepped out of a Neiman Marcus catalog, treated us like paying customers; anything we wanted to drink,from water to champagne; rolls and butter, corn soup, salad,spaghetti with sauce, poached pink salmon topped with pink caviar on a thin layer of steamed spinach, steak that you could cut with a fork with peppercorns atop, brocolli, carrots, mushrooms; and pale orange sherbert with pieces of rinds for dessert. Everything was very delicious. And for the first time in my life I had trouble with the silverware, all of which was on the right-hand side of my plate. There were eight pieces-- one regular table knife, two odd-shaped knives that looked akin to a sword (the butter knife was across the bread plate), a soup spoon, one teaspoon and three forks. No, we weren't paying customers. It cost 35,000 yen, the equivalent of about $278 in our money, per person, for dinner and a live jazz show. (At that time approximately 126 yen equalled one U.S. dollar.) Houston Person and his quintet, including Etta Jones, the vocalist, were sponsored on this tour to Tokyo by Kenji Arai, owner of the club where we were eating. This tall, handsome Japanese man owned two clubs, both called The Good Day Club. The first evening the band performed at one club and the entire rest of the time the performances were at the other club, both in Tokyo; except one Sunday when a bus picked us up at our hotel and took us to Gotemba, about two and a half hours out of Tokyo, where the band performed at what was called the Westgate English School, a school that was about to open for Japanese businessmen to learn to speak English. That Sunday, as well as each evening, the band was fed before their performance. And Jem and I were included. We were there in the first place because Jem and Etta are long-time friends and Jem decided we'd tag along with the group.

Incidentally, a van picked us up each evening and took us to the club. Good thing, because the streets in Tokyo seem to be laid out in no rhyme or reason and most only have the name written in Japanese. Houston said that Mr. Arai knew that we'd never find the place if we were on our own; not to mention the traffic jams.

Upon arriving at the club on a prior evening and hearing songs by Mahalia Jackson, I gave Mr. Arai, who was decked out in a tuxedo with a pale yellow ruffled shirt and a black bow tie, a quizzical look and said, "Mahalia Jackson???!" He didn't speak English, but he held up one finger intimating that Mahalia was his number one singer. I was flabbergasted because I thought Etta was his number one singer. Especially since he had just made a gorgeous ring with a cluster of what looked like diamonds and given it to Etta (Jewelry-making is his hobby). In fact, the evening before that he had observed the ring on Etta's hand and noticed that it was too large. So he beckoned for her to give it back to him. Etta relunctantly gave it up after one of the hostesses explained in English that he was going to adjust the ring and return it to her the next evening. And he did. But not only did he adjust it to fit her finger properly, he changed it from yellow gold to white gold to match the other rings that Etta wore.

All of us; Houston Person, the saxophonist/leader; Etta; Stan Hope, the pianist; Peter Weiss, the bassist; Birtell Knox, the drummer; Jem and myself left New York on November 12, 1990 via Japan Airlines on a DC 747 and arrived non-stop in Japan twelve hours and twenty-five minutes later, Jem and I having once again crossed the International Dateline. This was my first observation of the Japanese female catering totally to the male. At one point our cabin attendant was so intent on getting Jem whatever he wanted at the moment that my wants were almost forgotten. But when this happened I then became the recipient of graciousness never before shown to me.

Each seat in Executive Class was really a recliner equipped with a foot rest. And each passenger received two kits; one with a pair of plastic slippers and a shoe horn, and the other containing a toothbrush, toothpaste, a comb, tissues, a lint brush, BandAids, Q-tips, shoe polish, and black fabric eye shades to block out the light if you wanted to sleep at an odd time. We also received earphones to listen to different music channels or to hear the big screen TV; plus there was a small individual TV screen attached to each recliner where two movies were shown other than the one on the big screen. I enjoyed Pretty Woman and The Hunt For Red October. In addition, on our return trip they showed a sedentary exercise tape, and we participated.

Before each meal (we had two, plus two snacks) we were handed a steaming hot face cloth. And for lunch there was a choice of a Japanese lunch or western lunch. I chose the Japanese, Jem the western. I didn't like the taste of everything on my tray but I especially liked the grilled eel on steamed rice with Marron sauce. The tray was exceptionally attractive with many dainty food decorations. Snacks consisted of a black sealed package, one-half containing dry roasted mixed nuts as we know them and the other half containing beautifully decorated and shaped, glazed crunchy things that seemed like simulated nuts, some even covered with glazed seaweed. Some were round and hollow, some were flat and shaped like a tiny star, some were long like a bean; all pretty to look at and fascinating. I liked them, but I was more curious as to how they were made. I never did find out. The other snack was a dixie cup of Haagen Dazs vanilla ice cream. Dinner was western style.

Our very smooth flight ended at Narita Airport, some two hours from Tokyo, in 60-degree weather, where we deplaned on the air field and took buses with midget seats (most Japanese are tiny folk) to the terminal. A van was waiting for the members of the band but what with all the luggage and instruments there was only room for four people. But they did take our luggage, leaving us with just having to get ourselves to the hotel in Tokyo. We had heard about the high price of everything in Japan but reality set in when it cost us over 5000 yen (about $40) just to get from Narita Airport to Tokyo City Terminal in Tokyo, via bus, and then another 2700 yen (about $21) to get from Tokyo City Terminal to our hotel via taxi. Traffic drives on the left in Japan and tipping is not required or expected. There was no subway stop near our hotel, or we might have gone for it and it would have been a lot cheaper. The bus from Narita Airport to Tokyo City Terminal also had midget seats and there were public telephones in one area of the bus.

When we arrived at our hotel our luggage was already in the lobby, neatly covered with what looked like fish netting. And when we registered at the desk and learned that we would receive a ten per cent discount per night on our room, which had been reserved at 23,000 yen per night (approximately $181), we were overjoyed. We believe the discount came about because we were with the band. I had jokingly said to Etta and Houston on the plane that if anyone asked, I was Etta's wardrobe lady and Jem was Houston's valet.

Our room was a small efficiency room with a king-sized bed. There was a refrigerator stocked with beer, mineral water, sodas and juice. A shelf over the refrigerator held one electric burner, green tea,powdered tea and a two-cup teapot with two China cups (bowls) with covers. A radio was built into one night table that had one English-speaking station which played popular American music, a WPAT-type station; a Japanese-speaking station, a classical station and a shortwave Japanese station. The remote control for the TV had a bilingual button. All the English speaking movies could be heard either in English or Japanese. It was fun to flip the button from one to the other and hear and see familiar actors and actresses suddenly speaking Japanese. There were two pairs of soft vinyl slippers (one size fit all) and two kimonos. Each day we received fresh kimonos. And every morning there was an

English newspaper pushed under our door. Also, in one night table there were two books; a New Testament in English and Japanese, supplied by Gideons International in Japan, and the Teachings of Buddha in English and Japanese, supplied by the Buddhist Promoting Foundation.

Late one morning we kept hearing a bell. We thought it was the television. It turned out to be a doorbell. Each room had a doorbell. And it was so neatly done that you couldn't even notice it. A small square was cut in the wallpaper and when the square was pushed, the bell would ring. The floor captain was checking to see what time the maids could clean our room.

The stopper in the bathtub consisted of a chain with a hard rubber black ball on the end, eliminating the necessity to have a stopper the exact size of the drain. Also, the bathtub was sunken below the floor with an overflow area the entire length of the tub.

The lamps on the night tables were equipped with dimmer knobs. And one table contained the controls for all the lighting in the room as well as the TV and the air-conditioning/heating system. All these little details really made our stay very comfortable.

On our second day in Tokyo Jem couldn't walk. For fear of him spending the next ten days in bed, drastic measures were called for. At 8 a.m. I contacted the front desk and asked for an English-speaking doctor. Ten minutes later a doctor called. He sounded like an American. After informing the doctor that Jem thought it was a gout attack brought on by the long plane flight, the doctor said he would be at our room in an hour. Fifty minutes later the doctor called and said he had been delayed but would be at our room in twenty minutes. Twenty minutes later our doorbell rang and there stood Dr. Stin, a tall, slim man carrying a doctor's bag in one hand and a cordless telephone in the other. He came in, took Jem's blood pressure, manipulated the foot, drew a vial of blood from Jem's arm, gave him a shot of cortisone in the upper arm, directed him to take four Indocin tablets, which the doctor brought with him, and left enough Indocin for the remainder of our eleven-day stay in Japan. He promised Jem that if Jem did exactly what the doctor recommended, two tablets every four hours, Jem would be walking by 4 o'clock that day.

The doctor sat talking with us for a while and answering his phone whenever it would ring. When I said to him, "How 'd you end up in Japan?" he said that he was from the Bronx; that he had met a Japanese student in medical school in the States and that they had married and he returned to Japan with her. He's a one-man-visiting-doctor-service, and he speaks fluent Japanese. When we inquired about the bill he said his usual fee was about 25,000 yen and that it could be put on our hotel bill. But when we asked if there would be a problem if we paid him in American money, he hesitated and then said, "Okay, just give me $150," thus saving us about $50. He said he'd have Jem's blood tested and would give us a report and a paid bill before we returned to the States. (Jem was later fully reimbursed by his health plan back in the States.) About a half hour after the doctor left, the Assistant Hotel Manager called to see how Mr. Morton san was feeling. At 4:15 p.m. Dr. Stin called to see how Jem was doing, and Jem was walking. We were able to go to the club that night with the band.

Speaking of the club, or I should say clubs, both were tastefully and eloquently furnished, including bronze, brass, silver and alabaster busts of females, wall-to-wall hand-carved rugs of pastel floral design, gigantic vases of fresh cut flowers and a sound system that I believe could only be found in Tokyo, the electronics capitol of the world.

At one club, as you walked into the ladies room there were two sinks in a marble top just beneath a mirrored wall. In one corner of the marble top stood a huge vase with fresh cut flowers. On a wall to the right of the flowers was a cloth towel box. You know the kind where you pull down the towel to reach a clean area to dry your hands. Well, this box was automated. You merely pressed the box in a certain spot with one finger and this beautiful white and green linen towel automatically came down. You dried your hands and a second or two later the towel automatically disappeared in the box, leaving no slack towel in view, soiled or otherwise. To the right-hand side of the ladies room there was a black shiny door. The toilet was in there; black ebony trimmed in gold. On the left-hand side of the room there was a clear glass wall through which could be seen a red bathtub with gold fixtures. The soap reminded me of that round Christmas candy that has a floral design in the middle that goes completely through the candy, except the soap had an oval shape.

We always arrived at the club early because the band had to make a sound check. So we were able to observe the guests arriving. The men always walked in first and the ladies followed. We were told that they were all wealthy businessmen. Nothing was said about the women. We had gone on this trip with Houston Person's approval of course, and there were certain guidelines we were to follow. He told us never to walk into the club proper and just sit at a table because if we did it would cost us an arm and a leg. One evening Takao, the liaison between the band and the club owner, said to me: "Mr. Morton; what kind of work he do?" I said, "He used to work in the courts." (Jem retired in August) Takao said, "Court?" I replied, "He used to work with the judges." Takao said, "Ah, Judge!" Now whether this conversation brought us any preferential treatment down the line we'll probably never know. But on the following evening, as Jem and I walked into the club with the band, Takao motioned for the two of us only, not the rest of the band, to be seated at an empty dinner table. He said something in Japanese to the owner and still insisted that we sit down. As soon as we sat down several of the hostesses, who were used to seeing us with the band by now, came over and asked what we would like to drink. Now I don't even like champagne but the word flew out of my mouth. Jem echoed me. When the champagne was poured I took a sip and it was so smooth that I liked it. Jem winked at me and said, "Top shelf." I was one nervous wreck for about fifteen minutes.

First of all, we weren't dressed properly to be sitting with the other guests. We were looking good, but we didn't have on fancy clothes, and I was very self-conscious. I was also afraid that we would have to pay the so-called fee for entering and dining in the club, et cetera. Meantime the hostesses kept bringing us course after course. Seems like they were falling all over themselves waiting on us. For a moment I thought we were celebrities. Jem looked at me and said, "Relax, kid. If we have to pay, we'll use plastic money and pay for it later." Somehow I managed to relax and thoroughly enjoy the rest of the dinner as well as the rest of the evening. We never had to pay a penny, or a yen, by the way.

Takao was a real gentleman. He was the one who walked Etta on stage and waited for her when she had done her last number. He sometimes met us at our hotel and rode with us to the club. He also met us and rode with us on the bus to Gotemba. And his charming wife, Junko, also a singer and a friend of Etta's, came along with a a gorgeous gal who had spent ten years in Alaska but is now back in Tokyo and has her own club. Etta knew the two women from a prior Japanese tour and this time they came to one of the clubs to hear her.

Saturday evening before the Gotemba trip Takao walked us over to his wife's gig at an Irish-type bar not far from the club where we were. We had to almost fight our way through the streets, it was so crowded with people. His wife has a soft, sweet voice and she's good. She sang in English. The trio behind her was excellent. After the show I said to the bass player that I would love to take the piano player home with me. He translated what I said for the benefit of the piano player and the piano player got very excited. I don't know how it came out in the translation, but I think he liked it.

Tokyo fascinated me. Tokyo, where the cars stop to let you cross the street if there's no traffic light; where the cross-walk signs and exit signs are green instead of red; where there are hundreds of bicycles parked on the street all day and all night and no one steals them; where you can leave all of your belongings on your seat in the Bullet Train and go to the dining car, eat a meal, return to your seat in another car and find your belongings just as you left them; where Christmas decorations were on display in early November; where traditional Christmas music could be heard in McDonalds as you sat having pancakes; where geisha girls could be seen riding on the escalator in a shopping mall in the middle of the day; where the restaurants display plastic, colorful replicas of all the meals they serve and one orders by number, and when it arrives at your table it's exactly like the display; where a person wears a mask that covers their nose and mouth if they have a cold or if they work at a toll booth; where there's a Tokyo Disney Land, Toys-R-Us, a

Kentucky Fried Chicken and Tony Roma's Ribs; where most fresh fruits are giant size, grapes included; where the department stores have nurseries or play areas with attendants for children while the parents shop; where there's a Roman Catholic Church, an Anglican Episcopal Church, a Lutheran Church, a Baptist Church, but absolutely no Methodist Church; where when you say "Arigato" (which means thank-you in Japanese) to a Japanese they smile and bow profusely and say "Thank you, thank you" in English; and when you ask the hotel maid for whatever, she literally goes running to get it for you or to get someone who speaks or understands English.

One day we decided to take a train that was the equivalent of the Long Island railroad to the Ginza (Fifth avenue type) district. Etta confessed that she and Houston had tried to do this one day but got nowhere and ended up taking a taxi. But our fearless leader, Jem, said, "Ah, come on; we can do it." So we followed him across the wide, wide Takanawa Street to the train station. We somehow knew we had to purchase our tickets from a machine, but everything was written in Japanese or some other Asian language. So Jem said, "All right, stand here and try to look intelligent and someone will help us." A well-dressed Japanese man smiled at us and said, "May I help you?" He showed us how to work the machines and we got our tickets and went up on the platform. Our hotel had given us a little map showing The Ginza and how many stops it was from where we were. Incidentally, Etta and Jem are movie buffs and we were heading to see Goodfellas. Etta had an idea of where the movie was located. Through the stares and curious looks from the natives we made our way to The Ginza and found the movie, which was located on the seventh floor in an office building; a nice, neat, clean little movie house with great acoustics. The movie was in English with Japanese titles. Afterwards we found our way back to the train station, purchased our tickets as if we had been doing it for years, and took a train going in the wrong direction. But we soon discovered our mistake and corrected it.

I did not like the movie, but the public toilets in the movie house were out-a-sight. They were beautiful and spotless. There were several toilets like ours, what the Japanese call western style, and several Japanese style toilets, where there's actually no toilet bowl, just a hole in the center of the floor, for squatting. The door to each booth went all the way to the floor for ultimate privacy. And when one left the booth the door was left open with the lid down on the western style toilets. In a service stop on the road to Gotemba the toilets flushed automatically. I had encountered this once in the States and experienced the same reaction--a little frustrated. Everything was neat and clean though. Etta purchased a hot dog at this stop and brought it back to the bus. It was on a stick and there was no roll.

As our bus neared Gotemba we were able to see Mt. Fuji (an extinct volcano), the highest mountain in Japan. It was simply breathtaking.

When our bus pulled up at the English School in Gotemba, workmen seemed to be completing the grounds of the building. The band set up for a sound check, and the females in our group were assigned a room that looked like a classroom, save for a couch and a large television. The males were assigned a room with chairs and a long table. The rest of the rooms on the ground level were empty. Two hours later one empty room had been transformed into a dining room with formal setting, with candles yet and fresh flowers. Another room had been transformed into a nightclub setting.

At the dining table we were served appetizers of cheeses, caviar, olives and fancy crackers, followed by a turkey dinner, served by the same hostesses that were at the Good Day Clubs. And they had not traveled with us on our bus. After dinner the band performed for the distinguished people in the makeshift nightclub, a crowd much like the people at The Good Day Clubs in Tokyo. The President of the Westgate English School, a wealthy Japanese man, was the loudest in the crowd. He sat next to me at one point, put his arm around my chair and said to me, "They think I'm a little crazy because I'm wearing a tuxedo with jogging shoes."

Before the band performed, the fellows were loud and boisterous, playing poker in their room. And I was in there at the time playing two-handed pinochle with Stan. A short, stout, white female poked her head in the door and said, "Now, that's good old American laughter!" She was homesick, from the States, and was a teacher at the school. Her statement gave us food for thought.

Another white female approached me in the hallway later where I was waiting to escort Etta from the bathroom. She introduced herself as Louise and said she was from Seattle and that she was going to be a teacher at the school. As we stood talking, Etta exited the bathroom and walked towards us. I introduced Louise to Etta saying, "Louise, this is Etta Jones." Louise's eyes grew as wide as saucers. She looked dumbfounded but finally managed to say, "No way, no way!" It took Etta and me a few seconds to realize that Louise was expressing her surprise and pleasure at meeting THE ETTA JONES. Louise then blurted out, "I listen to you all the time-- I have your records. I always hear you on 'so and so's' radio station. No way." Louise's smile grew broader. She looked at Etta with such admiration that Etta seemed embarrassed. Louise continued, "Do you know how famous you are?" Etta laughed and said, "No." After the show Louise came back to Etta's dressing room with another female teacher. They both got autographs. It was a lovely day, filled with new friends and new experiences.

Jem and I took a side trip to Kyoto, the old capital, for a one-day tour. It cost approximately $700. This required our getting up at 4:30 a.m. to catch a train across the street from our hotel that would take us to the Bullet Train, which would get us to Kyoto in time to meet our tour group at a hotel in Kyoto. There were no bums on the platforms and the platforms were immaculate. There were food stands on the platforms that were just opening, and people were purchasing breakfast, which they took on the train, pulled down a tray in front of their seat and spread out their breakfast. Japan is filled with people comforts.

When we changed trains and got settled on the Bullet Train we had breakfast in the dining car as we watched the landscape go by so fast we weren't aware of what it was that we saw. Two hours later we were in Kyoto joining our chosen tour.

Kyoto is full of Japanese history, with its many shrines and temples; where we learned that both religions, Buddism and Shintoism are exercised at the same time by many Japanese; where we saw a giant candle monument, a tribute to Buddism, symbolizing that Buddism is the light of the world.

During our lunch break while on the tour in Kyoto a young, white American male latched onto Jem and me. He was from New Orleans and was in Japan visiting a buddy from the service who married a Japanese girl. He was so caught up with the beautiful Japanese girls that he told us he couldn't wait to get back to New Orleans to let his mother know he was moving to Japan to take a job teaching English. He said he had never seen such beautiful women.

On our last evening in Tokyo the band was hot. The session had been recorded and everyone had been caught up in the music. After the last bow, each member of the band was handed an oversized bouquet of fresh flowers. I inherited the drummer's because he didn't want "no flowers." But we couldn't bring them on the plane so we had to leave them for the hotel maids, but not before I took lots of pictures.

Next morning, bright and early, we met in the hotel lobby where we checked out and Takao greeted us as we entered our big bus for the trip to the airport. Good thing he was accompanying us because entrance to Narita Airport grounds calls for a physical search of all persons and luggage. But because Takao was with us and vouched for us, we only had to be counted and show our passports.

Just before our plane taxied down the runway Jem exclaimed, "I never saw anything like this in my life! Ellie, take a look out the window." I leaned across him and saw the entire ground crew lined up side by side waving our plane good-bye.

Back home, at Kennedy Airport, when we went through Customs we were merely asked, "Where are you coming from?" And when we said, "Tokyo," we were waved through the gate. Not one bag was searched! While still at the airport we exchanged our left-over yen for American dollars and received more than we expected.

Recently a friend said to me, "Ellie, out of all the fabulous trips you've taken, what's the place you'd like to return to?" and without a second's hesitation I said, "Japan."

* * *

MY COUSIN VIVVIE IN ALASKA

When cousin Vivvie, who's in the undertaker business in Bradenton, Florida first learned through her brother in Richmond, Virginia, that Jem and I were planning to go to Alaska, she called to ask if she could go with us; and we said yes. Vivvie and I were very close as children but have drifted apart through the years. She's nine months older than I am.

After many phone calls and price quotings, we agreed that the three of us would share an outside stateroom, one upper bed and two lower, on the Dolphin Deck of the Dawn Princess cruise ship; that we would fly from Kennedy Airport in New York to Seattle, Washington and from Seattle, Washington to Vancouver, Canada, where we would board our ship and cruise for one week along the inside passage for seven days, from Vancouver to Whittier, Alaska. We were to also spend a week in Anchorage on our own.

To avoid any mix-up of plane arrivals, et cetera, Vivvie arrived in New York a few days early so that we three could set out on our journey together. Before leaving Florida she mailed a box to my house containing her New York wardrobe. She brought with her lots of cash (doesn't believe in credit cards), a suitcase full of cruise wear, another suitcase full of Alaska-wear, and a fully packed carry-on bag of medicine, makeup, and cans of snuff.

She and I had fun visiting with family here in New York before embarking on our vacation, but here at the house it was evident that she was Miss Anne and I was the maid. And since it was only for a short time, I played the game.

Our travel connections on August 31, 1991 were excellent. Buses were awaiting our arrival at the Vancouver Airport to carry us directly to the ship. Vancouver is Canada's third largest city and is very cosmopolitan.

Once aboard ship, we were escorted to our stateroom. When we saw the size of it we wanted to cry. We tried to switch rooms or obtain a single room for Vivvie but the entire ship was completely booked. When Vivvie and I calmed down (because Jem was cool) we realized there really was space for us and all the luggage, especially if some of it was unpacked. We certainly didn't plan to spend much time in the room, and we didn't. So, the room situation worked out well.

This was my fourth cruise, but a first for Jem and Vivvie. And the three of us went our separate way mostly, except for mealtimes when we shared seating assignments in the dining room, and the same waiter and busboy throughout the entire cruise. To our dismay this turned into one big embarrassment for Jem and I. Vivvie acted like a nouveau riche and demanded service, driving our waiter crazy, driving the busboy crazy and driving us crazy. She demanded dishes that were not on the menu, she demanded water every few minutes, she complained about this and complained about that. She talked about the food, but she ate everything they set in front of her. And in her demanding and receiving whatever, she never said "Thank-you." One day she made the busboy so nervous that he dropped a glass of water that he was about to place in front of her, narrowly missing her. She failed to show up for one meal and I don't know who was happier, the waiter, the busboy, or us. We found out later that she had gone to the wrong dining room.

She has a close friend back in Bradenton named Constine who could not make the trip with her. But he might as well have been there because she talked about him incessantly and called him on the phone, from the ship or the shore, at least once a day. And although she claimed she was so tired and had to get away from her business, she also called the funeral parlor every day. I think she got a kick out of yelling at the ship's telephone officer to get whatever telephone number she wanted next and to ring her back in our room. I wish I could have seen her telephone bill.

Every evening, before retiring, she rang the bell for our steward and demanded a pitcher of ice water. And when the steward returned with the water she'd say, "Put it over there." Yes, Queen Vivian was having the time of her life.

On our fourth day at sea the ship's loudspeaker blared that we were passing near a glacier. And I ran on deck with everyone else, in the rain, to take a picture. My first glacier! My mouth dropped open and I froze where I stood, forgetting the camera hanging around my neck. There it was. A gigantic mountain of ice with a core of blue. Even as we watched, pieces of the mountain broke off and floated into the water; big pieces, medium sized pieces, tiny pieces. What a mind-boggle to even imagine that this glacier started as fresh snow maybe ten thousand years ago.

It rained every day but there was still plenty to do aboard ship. I attended a couple of early morning interdenominational church services in the chapel, which doubled as a movie theatre; saw a couple of good movies, played the slots a little in the casino, took Italian lessons, visited the library, played bridge, sang on two evenings (once in the piano lounge and once in a different lounge where they featured a Karoake SingAlong.) The Karoake was fun because you were made into a recording star. Everything was provided-- the words, the musical accompaniment, the audience, the lights, and the recording equipment. I sang Moon River. After this, people would approach me wherever I went on the ship and say, "Aren't you the one who sang?" All told, there were only six blacks on board, three of whom were females!

Jem and I kept running into a man on deck who reminded me of an American Indian. We had long talks with him. During one of our talks he told us that he was of the Baha'i faith, which teaches reformation of oneself, and that he was the entertainer in the ship's lounge, playing requests on the piano and also singing. And believe it or not, his name is Bob Bellows. Jem let him know that I sing a little, so Bob invited me to sing. That's how it came about that I sang in the piano lounge. Vivvie missed both of my performances. Bob made a promise to contact us in New York in November 1992 when he would be here for the Ba'Hai convention.

I would run into Vivvie now and then. She'd either be sitting reading her bible or preaching wherever she could catch an ear, or just walking along carrying that heavy carry-on briefcase filled with medicine and things wrapped in little pieces of tinfoil. She claimed nothing was wrong with her physically but she took medication all day and at specific times. The first day or so she got turned around and couldn't find our room, but that didn't last. After all, she had to get to the phone. She asked me to show her how to play the slots one day. I'm not so sure she didn't already know. I just knew Miss Moneybags would hit a jackpot. But she didn't.

Our first stop was Ketchikan, Alaska's "First City" because it's the first major community travelers see as they journey north. It started as an Indian fishing camp and is now known for its fishing and timber industries, and has the world's largest collection of Totem Poles. We went ashore for a few hours and shopped and took lots of pictures. The city seemed quaint, surrounded by mountains, hilly, with a lot of wooden steps to climb. The harbor was loaded with small boats and a few seaplanes -- but beautiful. If ever I make this trip again I'll know to do all my shopping in Ketchikan because, too late, I realized the best prices were there.

Our next stop was Juneau, the largest city in the United States and the only state capital accessible only by air or water because no roads connect it with the rest of the world. Millions of dollars in gold was mined in Juneau by the end of World War II and then the business of government took over.

When we went ashore we became interested in a tour. While trying to decide what to do, a van pulled up with a black driver whose tour consisted of more hours than we had ashore. It was so rare to see a black that I was full of questions for him. He answered all of them cheerfully and the most remarkable information I gleaned was that he originally lived in Elizabeth City, North Carolina, thirty miles from my hometown of Plymouth! While still talking to the driver of the van a sleek black limousine pulled up. Its driver was a young black man, with a Jeri Curl no less, and we made a deal with him for an hour tour. This fellow was from Virginia and had been in Juneau for ten years. Vivvie wanted to make phone calls from ths shore, so she did not go with us. It was nice having a private tour of the city as well as a trip to the famous Mendenhall Glacier, where we reached out and touched the ice. Helicopters were hovering over the top and once in a while a helicopter would land and let the passengers walk out on the glacier. But we were not so venturesome.

Skagway, our next stop, was the most depressing place I've ever seen. I suppose the rainy weather didn't help either. It might have been the gateway to the gold fields and the shortest route to the Klondike years ago but it's like a muddy ghost town now with a couple of abandoned railroad tracks, and in the distance, from our ship, could be seen the steeple of a Russian-type church. The three of us went ashore for a hot minute; Vivvie went in search of a telephone, and Jem and I returned to the ship. The most impressive thing about Skagway for me was the massive mountain that greeted us as our ship docked. It was covered with all kind of names written in bright colors and written up so high on the mountain that it made you wonder how it was done. We did not dock at Glacier Bay or at the College Fjords (narrow inlets of the sea between cliffs or steep slopes, and usually misty) but each place was pointed out to us. And on we sailed to Whittier, the last port for our ship. As we pulled into Whittier, around midnight, while watching the activity down on the dock from our deck, a young white male did a double take upon seeing Jem and I and he blurted out, "Did y'all just come aboard?" It was obvious that he hadn't noticed us all week.

The next morning we bid goodbye to the crew and together with all the other passengers we walked a short distance to a waiting doubledecker train which was to take us to Anchorage. All three of us sat upstairs, but not together. Vivvie always seemed to be lagging behind, so we stopped waiting for her. We each carried our own small luggage and souvenirs but Vivvie had so much more than she could easily handle. She sometimes acted helpless and ignorant but we soon found that this was a put-on.

Our view from the top of the train was simply spectacular. It was only then that I fully realized the vastness and the beauty of the Alaskan wilderness; the distant mountains covered with snow, the plush greenery alongside the railroad; a fisherman here and there standing in thigh-high boots fishing in tall, grassy water.

This was our only way to travel as a group from Whittier to Anchorage because there were no connecting roads. At the first town we reached we were shown another railroad, with flatbed cars only, where trucks and cars were loading to go into Whittier or any other little town along the railroad.

Our guide on the train pointed out many things, among which were the dali sheep on a mountain; the area where the 1964 earthquake struck and; just before pulling into Anchorage, a town where there was an airplane in every back yard.

In Anchorage there was a bus waiting to take us to our motel. At last Vivvie was going to have her own room and her own private telephone. As soon as we settled in I called her room, which was right next to ours. Yes, her line was busy. I reached her a short time later and asked whether she wanted to go to dinner with us. Her reply was, "Gee, I just took a pill and I can't eat for 40 minutes. Can you wait till then?" I said, "No! Bye!" So Jem and I hung together and Vivvie was still on her own.

We were to spend a week in Anchorage. Long before leaving New York I tried to contact Andonia and George, who reside in Anchorage, although we had never met. Actually, George's sister is married to Vivvie's brother in Richmond, Virginia, but Vivvie had never met them either.

In all my phone conversations between Anchorage and New York, when our trip was in the planning stage, I was only able to catch up with George. And when our trip was finalized and I talked to George, telling him where we would be staying in Anchorage, he said, "I'll be out of town when you arrive, but I'm sure my wife will be here."

I rang his wife after dinner on Saturday, the day of our arrival. No luck. After two tries I gave up and said I'd try again on Sunday. Around 9 p.m. Saturday evening our phone rang and a female voice who introduced herself as Loretta said that she was Andonia's best friend; that Andonia had to go out of town also and that Loretta had just received a call from Las Vegas, from

Andonia, asking her to contact us to see if we wanted to go to church with Loretta on Sunday morning. Andonia was to return to Anchorage late Sunday evening. Loretta said she'd pick us up at 9 a.m. on Sunday morning.

By 8:45 a.m. Sunday morning Jem and I were standing outside our motel waiting for Loretta, as planned. Vivvie was not interested in going with us. At 9:20 when Loretta had not shown, I called her from the motel lobby and the conversation went like this: "Is this Loretta J?" "Yes." "This is Eleanor Speer from New York." Silence. "You promised to pick us up at 9 a.m. and take us to church with you." "Yes; but it's not 9 o'clock yet." "It's 9:20!" "Oh my goodness; it is?" "Yes!" "I'm so sorry; I forgot to set my clock. How embarrassing! I'll be there as soon as I can. Please go back to your room and I'll call you from the lobby when I arrive."

Loretta is a school teacher and also the President of the NAACP in Anchorage. And I don't think she'll ever forgive herself for the snafu. And we did get to church on time that Sunday. Jem received permission to videotape the service of the Baptist Church. I wanted to sing a solo but the organist was very firm with Loretta in telling her it was the young people's service and they had lots of music to do. Loretta was really beside herself at this.

We had introduced ourselves to Loretta as Eleanor Speer and James Morton when she picked us up at the motel. But at the church she mistakenly introduced us as Mr. and Mrs. Speer. So when the minister asked the visitors to stand and give their name and where they were from and Loretta nudged me I stood and complied. The next thing I heard from across the church was, "I'm James Speer from Jamaica, New York." Other than that, the service was uneventful.

Afterwards we took Loretta to lunch at a fancy down-town hotel restaurant. Over lunch we talked and talked and then Loretta asked if we had any kids. I looked at Jem and he looked at me.
I said, "We'd better tell her;" meaning the truth about our names. When we told her about the mix-up at church she became so flustered that we ordered her another drink of wine. We sat talking

for hours, feeling like we had known Loretta all our lives. Before the day ended she took us to her spanking new NAACP offices and then returned us to our motel, where we filled Vivvie in on all that she missed. She had eaten twice and had gone shopping for more postcards and souvenirs. Andonia reached us after she arrived at work on Monday, and she took the three of us to dinner, together with Loretta, that evening. Andonia is a tall, lovely, unassuming young lady. She contacted us early each day and really made our stay in Anchorage very special. When she didn't take us to dinner, we took her and Loretta. One evening Andonia picked us up in her RV (recreational vehicle motorhome). We dined at a soul food restaurant and afterwards were given a grand city tour of Anchorage, including driving by several fine homes which were built by her husband, who is in the construction business.

When Andonia found out that my birthday was on the Thursday of that week she invited us to her home for dinner at 8 p.m. And she sent a car to pick us up. When we arrived, there were eight additional dinner guests, including their daughter. After working all day on the job, Andonia and Loretta cooked and served capon, pig feet, greens, red beans, lima beans, white potatoes, baked sweet potatoes, spaghetti, hot bread, lemonade and champagne. Before the dessert was served a huge, decorated candle was lit and brought for me to blow out and everyone sang Happy Birthday. Every time I think about this I get goose pimples, remembering that these beautiful strangers went to all this trouble to celebrate my birthday in Alaska. Then came the dessert of peach cobbler, sweet potato pie, chocolate cake and grapes.

We never did get to meet George because he was still out of town. They have a most unusually beautiful home on a hill, with several fireplaces and several terraces, way out in the suburbs where the nearest neighbor is approximately a mile away. They also have a big, friendly Boxer.

In Anchorage the hotel tax is 8-1/2 per cent, but there is no sales tax. I felt like I was in a foreign country. And local phone calls are only fifteen cents. Guess that's because the telephone company is owned by Alaska. The railroad is also owned by Alaska. Premium gasoline is only $1.18 per gallon, thanks to their oil refinery and the TransAtlantic pipeline. The natives, Eskimos and Indians, receive a subsistence from the government, plus free hospitalization. The Eskimos seem shy or standoffish but the Indians are super friendly.

Most homes are built of wood even though their winters are very cold. Bricks would be much too expensive since they would have to be imported. Food and liquor is very high compared to New York, but the huge supermarkets are fantabulous, with mostly everything under one roof. We found the most beautiful and tastiest fruits and vegetables. Breakfast, in our motel coffee shop, of oatmeal, toast and coffee came to $4.65. And all the breakfast menus carry reindeer sausages, which taste like Polish sausages to me. I would have preferred them for dinner. One of the waitresses in the coffee shop was a young black woman who left Brooklyn and went to Anchorage to raise her son. It worked out well so far, so she said.

The help in our motel was mainly Eskimo and Indian. Ten per cent of the population in Anchorage (approximately 250,000) is black and most of them are civil servants, including Andonia. Alaskans are not required to pay income tax. Most blacks that we came in contact with were from the southern states of North America; the whites were mostly from the northeastern states.

Alaska (Alieska) consists of a half million square miles and five thousand glaciers, and was purchased from Russia in 1867 for seven million dollars, the equivalent of less than two cents an acre. It is three thousand miles from east to west, and roads are almost nonexistent.

On a bright, clear day in Anchorage you can hear the residents proudly say, "The mountain is out today;" referring to Mt. McKinley, the highest mountain in America. It is a breathtaking sight.

During the portion of our return flight from Vancouver to Seattle, Vivvie, Jem and I were not able to sit with one another. I ended up on the middle seat in a row of three, between an elderly white man at the window seat and an elderly white woman seated on the aisle. He kept making small talk with me. She was busy reading a book. When the airline attendant came offering refreshments I found out they were together, husband and wife, as it turned out. The wife finally asked where I was heading. When I said New York she closed her book and told me their life story. Well, just partly. They were heading for a small town in California where they now live but they had lived for many years in New York City and she said she wished that she could crawl into my luggage and return to New York with me; that at least once a year she makes sure to get back to New York; that she stays with her sister-in-law in the city and looks forward to that visit of a week; attending a religious conference.

Vivvie returned to New York with us and spent only two more days, mainly because she couldn't wait to see her Constine. And in spite of everything I believe she had the trip of her lifetime.

I would like to return to Alaska during May, June or July when it's the " Land of the Midnight Sun;" when they have three months of sunshine 24 hours a day; when children play in the street until midnight.

Epilogue:

1. To date, Nov. 12, 1992, we have received three postcards from Bob Bellows informing us that he and his wife will be in New York November 19 through the 26th. He's given us the name of his hotel and the phone number, and is anxious for us to meet his wife. We can hardly wait!

2. Around Valentine's Day, 1992 we received a call from George, here in New York. He, Andonia and Loretta were here for the weekend attending an NAACP conference. They managed to catch up with us via telephone on the evening before they were to leave New York. We picked them up at their hotel and took them to a Lebanese restaurant for dinner, in Brooklyn, a restaurant where you can take your own alcoholic beverage. We took champagne. So we finally met George, and he's a fun character. After dinner

Jem gave them a night tour of Harlem and further uptown. He showed them parts of New York that I had never seen. We had fun.

FRENCH FRANCS FOR A MARS BAR

It's early evening September 20, 1992 and we're at Kennedy Airport heading for Cairo, with a short stop in Paris to pick up connecting passengers. It took six hours to reach Paris and another four to Cairo.

Having booked our tour through Saga Holidays, Ltd., their representatives were waiting for us at the Cairo Airport, recognizing the ID tags that we wore and guiding us through customs and then to our bus to carry us to our first hotel. As we exited the airport on September 21, 1991 a smiling, dark-skinned Egyptian male looked at us and said, "Welcome, Nubians!"

We smiled and said, "Thank you!" Someone outside the airport beckoned and reached for our little carry-on bags, indicating that he would carry them to the bus fifteen feet away, but even in the blistering midday sun we declined; only to learn by the end of our trip that people from some of the poor families dash at tourists and wealthy Egyptians alike offering little service with confident insistence on a few small coins in return. As the bus became three-quarters full we saw for the first time the people with whom we would be spending the next fifteen days; all of us senior citizens, myself looking like the youngest, and Jim and I the only Nubians.

Before our bus pulled off, a tall, pale, handsome, innocent looking young man came aboard and, in a very clipped British accent, introduced himself as Tim Lane Stott, our tour manager. He handed each of us an envelope containing three Xeroxed sheets, the first of which welcomed us and told us that he would be with us throughout our time in Egypt, and additional information with regard to our next 24 hours, i.e. health hints, and money exchange information (Egyptian Pound 2.23 = one US dollar). The second page listed our itinerary for the next fifteen days. And the third page was a map of egypt displaying just the area where we would be traveling.

Our bus pulled away from the airport, and as far as my eyes could see there was only dry, scorched earth. I thought to myself, "You're in the desert now; what did you expect?!" But the dry outskirts very soon became the busy city streets of Cairo; a small area resembling the beautifully landscaped business area of any large city with tall office buildings, apartment buildings and luxury hotels which, all too soon, gave way to a crowded, noisy, disorderly city filled with veiled women in dark, long, flowing gowns with their heads covered in intricately folded scarves; a large proportion of men wearing galabeyas, the traditional loose-fitting Egyptian garment that looks like a nightgown; roadways filled with donkeys, bikes, motor bikes, motorcycles, pedestrians and vehicles (mostly Mercedes); where motorists drive to the left with one hand on the horn and where they sometimes stop on the green light and go on the red.

Tim told us what we thought at first to be Egyptian humor. For instance, a tourist once tried to hire a car to take him someplace and the driver said, "The car won't go because the horn is broken." What the driver really meant was that you cannot drive a car in Cairo without the use of the horn. It's so crowded that you lean on the horn all the way. Or a similar story where the driver said, "The car won't go because the lights don't work." In that instance the driver was being asked to drive someone out in an area where there were no street lights and, even though it was daylight at the time, the driver didn't want to go to a place where he would not be able to see at night.

We were heading for Mena House, our hotel for the night. Along the way I noticed clothes drying on terraces of beautiful buildings, a practice prevalent in most foreign countries; parked cars with a cover on them (which practice probably originated in Egypt because of all the dust from the desert); roadside stands of roasting corn; small children being carried straddling the shoulders of grownups; what looked like fall clothing in store windows; and a lot of men in white uniforms surrounding fenced-in buildings.

Our room at Mena House resembled one in a spacious palace, with high ceilings, lots of mahogany woodwork and a tiny balcony from which, after dark, we could see a fireworks display. After we dined with our group we returned to our room and then decided to roam around the hotel and its grounds. As we were leaving our room a man approached us from across the hall and asked if we would like to see the suite that he was tidying at the time. It turned out to be two rooms at $500.00 U.S. dollars per day, and of course it was fabulous. From that balcony we looked directly at the pyramids, which at night seemed almost to be in a calm and peaceful mystic glow; in direct contrast to the busy-ness of the rest of Cairo. Yes, we gave the man a tip. The following day, Tuesday, September 22nd, after breakfast we were introduced to Abdul, our tour guide, as distinguished from Tim, our tour manager, and we flew to Luxor where we dined and stayed overnight at Hotel Isis. The hotel greeted us with a drink of Hibiscus Tea with orange juice. Very refreshing. Our room was a postage stamp, but we had a panoramic view of the Nile River as well as all the hotel swimming pools, etc.

Wednesday, September 23rd, early morning we transferred via bus to our Oberoi Cruise Ship, the Scheherazad. And after lunch our bus took us to the mighty columns at the Temples of Karnak and Luxor. Late that evening we sailed up the Nile to Quina. Next day we visited Dendara and Abydos Temples in Quina and sailed back to Luxor.

I was never aware of what the exact temperature was during the day, only that it was terribly hot wandering through the temples in the dirt and the rocks, even with a hat, our all-cotton clothing and comfortable shoes. But in the evening I needed a sweater.

Our cabin aboard ship was adequate and the picture window showed the Nile in its serenity and splendor. We passed green farms, towns, minarets (a slender tower attached to a mosque and surrounded by one or more balconies from which the Muslim crier calls the hour of daily prayers), date trees, corn and millet. It was good to be away from the brown scorched earth and feast our eyes on the fine greenery along the Nile. We were told that in ancient times you could die of thrist ten miles on either side of the Nile and theoretically that's true today.

On Thursday, September 24, when we left our ship and boarded the bus that was to take us to Dendara and Abydos Temples, four new people joined us, bringing our total to 33. They sat across the back of the bus. Tim introduced them, telling us that they had joined our tour during the night before, having flown from Quebec. One was a missionary/nun (not wearing a habit), her sister, her niece and the niece's husband. They spoke French among themselves but spoke English to our group. The young couple acted like they were on their honeymoon. But when nosey me inquired, the husband told me they had been married for two years. He was very handsome and she was very shy, with a beautiful figure and complexion. She wore no makeup. Her English was not too good and whenever I tried to talk to her she blushed. Her nun/aunt was a real live wire-- a thin little lady who wore her French-fabric clothing well. The bus trip revealed children waving to us on their way to school, Egrets, donkeys, water buffalo, goats, camels, bicycles, motorcycles, motor bikes, river villages, unfinished houses, date trees, corn, millet and cotton. After visiting the temples our bus returned us to the ship. At dinner we shared a table with the folks from Canada. I managed four words in French and they laughed but seemed pleased. After dinner I sat on the top deck under the stars. It was so comfortable and beautiful that I fell asleep, only to be awakened by the noise from a young German group that was living it up at the other end of the deck.

In the middle of the night, even though I ate no fresh fruits or vegetables and drank only bottled water, I developed diarrhea. Tim had warned us that if we did get ill not to take medication that we brought with us from the States because it didn't work in Egypt but to call him any hour and he would bring us medication that would work. And since Tim had worked as a nurse in Egypt for several years, I listened to him. I called him about 2 a.m. He came and gave me medication and I was a lot better next day. But just as I thought I was okay I got ill again. Tim called the doctor. The doctor came, examined me and gave me additional medication. I was as good as new in two days. Although the doctor was the head of a hospital, his fee was $40 U.S. (which was reimbursed by Saga Holidays Travel Insurance.) Later I heard that nearly everyone in our group got sick at the same time I did.

On Friday, September 25th, back in Luxor, with the ship as our hotel now, after breakfast we stepped from our cruise ship directly onto a ferry on the Nile, which took us a short distance across the Nile to the west bank where we boarded a bus that took us to the Valley of the Artista who made the many reliefs or hieroglyphics (detailed sculptured forms and figures and ornaments), and the village of the workers. The most colorful tomb was one built and dedicated to the common worker, who must have been a midget and the work must have been done by other midgets because the steps were so narrow and the space where the tiny tomb sat was so small, and the weather so hot that I found it claustrophobic. The houses of this village were low, flat rectangles of dry mud, resembling a maze.

From this village the bus took us to the Valley of the Kings and Queens. After walking a short, hot distance in the desert sand, we crawled down hundreds of wooden steps along walls covered with thousands of reliefs. It was hard to comprehend that these reliefs were made by hand many, many years ago and that the colors were still so vibrant. Such intricate detail, such elaborate drawings and carvings, such beauty, such symbolism, such time-consuming and tedious work, such storytelling, such talent, such imagination, such pride.

Other reliefs that really stood out were those on the walls of the tomb of Queen Nefertari. Incidentally, flash cameras and video cameras were only allowed in most of the tombs if you paid a heavy fee. So very few, if any in our group, even carried their cameras into the tombs. We checked them at the entrances.

When we returned to the ferry I sat beside a gal who said she was traveling with a singles' tour from London, mostly females; said the tour travels to a different country each year. She was very friendly. We ran into each other again in Alexandria.

Today I became acutely aware that some hucksters are nasty or turn nasty when you refuse their merchandise or try to ignore them. I kept saying "No" to one and finally he very arrogantly said, "Goodbye!" The children wave to the busloads of tourists. Then they stretch out one hand in a begging manner and put their other hand to their mouth as if eating something, hoping that you will give them money or buy whatever they have for sale. If you don't acquiesce, they make faces at you.

Saturday, September 26th, we had an after-breakfast walk ashore to visit Esna Temple. The walk was neither short nor long but Jim hired a horse-drawn carriage (taxi) to return us to the ship. In order to reach where the taxis were we had to walk through a market. I spotted a very fashionable young black woman. We spoke and I asked where she was from. "Jamaica, West Indies" was her reply. And she warned me about the prices of whatever I might buy.

Our ship went through a canal between Esna and Edfu. And while the ship was being raised and then lowered in the lock we had plenty opportunity to gaze at the local people while they gazed back at us. I saw two men dressed in galabeyas walking along the street holding hands. I was told that this did not necessarily mean what I thought it meant; but that it was the custom in Egypt with any two men who are just plain friends. After going through the lock we sailed to Edfu and as we went ashore there were more horse-drawn carriages waiting to take us to Edfu Temple (four people to a carriage). All the way to the temple we were chased by children begging for pens. Other than that, it was a pleasant ride. As I listened to the sound of the trotting horses, I thought I was an extra in Quo Vadis!

Right after lunch this same day Abdul met with the group and explained that it was customary for each group aboard ship to compete in a sketch one evening; that this was the evening, and that it was scheduled for 9:30. He told us that there were four other travel groups aboard; two Spanish, one French and one German; and that we had to pick a theme for our sketch. He threw out three ideas and we agreed on one. All the characters were chosen: A pharaoh, pharaoh's assistant, pharaoh's two wives, his daughter, his court attendants, a doctor, a doctor's assistant, an embalmer, and many professional mourners. Abdul told everyone what costume they needed and that if they didn't have a galabeya and couldn't afford to buy one on the ship, that they could rent one for the evening from the ship's gift shop or he and Tim would help them make a costume.

Our sketch was to be that pharaoh's only daughter had died and pharaoh was searching for someone to bring her back to life because he couldn't live without her.

The ship was filled with activity all afternoon. There was a run on the gift shop and a run on galabeyas. Jim purchased a black galabeya trimmed in yellow and also bought a katina (head gear of red and white checks resembling a table cloth) and a black woven cord to tie around the cloth to hold it on his head. After all, he was chosen to be pharaoh and he had to look the part.

Dinner was never eaten so fast as on this evening. Everyone rushed from the dining room to transform themselves into their character. After helping Jim get into his costume I put on my black silk jump suit with a black, white and tan scarf and wandered up to the lounge deck with my video camera in time to find Tim and Abdul mummifying pharaoh's daughter by wrapping her entire body in toilet tissue. Her face was all made up and she lay stiff as a board. The doctor's assistant was helping him into his huge green smock and someone had made a giant hypodermic needle which the doctor carried. The front of his smock had a big white cross on it. His head was wrapped in a white band. The embalmer was gaunt enough in his pale makeup. The mourners (all female) were decked out in their fancy and colorful galabeyas but each had their head covered with a black scarf.

The first group to perform was from Spain and they did their sketch in Spanish; a sketch involving a pharaoh, too, but with a different twist from ours. They were very good. Our group was the next to perform. And our sketch began with Tim and Abdul bringing in the stretcher bearing pharaoh's daughter's body and laying it in front of pharaoh. Pharoah is seated, flanked by his two wives. He ad libs, as does all the other characters, asking for a doctor to come and try to revive his daughter.

The doctor and his assistant enter. Pharaoh orders them to bring his daughter back from death. But before the doctor and his assistant even attempt to do anything they begin haggling with pharaoh about their fee for the house call. Pharoah becomes incensed and has them thrown out of the palace.

The embalmer was next. He told pharaoh there was absolutely nothing he could do unless he was paid a fee in advance. He also was thrown out of the palace. Pharaoh then suggested that if all who remained would dance, perhaps his daughter would come alive again since she had loved dancing so very much when she was alive. Suddenly, lively music is heard. The mourners shed their black head scarves and the merriment begins. Through my video camera I notice a very beautiful young thing dancing vigorously and gracefully with our group of seniors and thought to myself that one of the Spanish girls just couldn't resist the music and decided to join us. What a figure, what a face, what agility. I heard the next day that this was the nun's niece. I truly did not recognize her.

The mourners and court attendants danced and danced. And oh so slowly the mummy began to move. She got up off the stretcher and started to dance. She danced and she danced. And they all lived happily ever after.

The next day our pharaoh's wife #1 expressed out loud that she felt that more attention should have been paid to her by pharaoh. And she seemed upset. Heretofore she had been warm and friendly.

The German group declined to do a sketch. But the remaining Spanish group and the French group did similar sketches. The one I liked best was done in pantomime by the French group. It seems their pharoah was melancholy and no one could cheer him up.

The doctor found absolutely nothing wrong with him. Pharaoh refused to eat, even his favorite foods. He would have nothing to do with his wives. The local dancing girls did not cheer him. But along came one particular dancer who was really built and pharoah seemed to perk up a little. As the dancer performed, pharaoh jumped from his throne, picked the dancer up in his arms and ran off stage with a great big grin on his face. The dancer was a male.

When the sketches were completed, each member of each group received a gift. Jim-- I mean our pharaoh received an ankh (a cross with a loop for its upper vertical arm and serving, especially in ancient Egypt, as an emblem of life). Immediately after the gift-giving, six workers on the ship entertained the audience with drums and a sort of sing-along where they sang a native phrase and we repeated after them. Then everybody formed one great long conga line. Nice party!

Very late that evening the folks from Quebec left our ship and flew to Alexandria.

On Sunday, September' 27, we went ashore after breakfast and walked to Kom Ombo Temple. It was a very comfortable morning weatherwise. On the way to the temple we passed a beautiful green vegetable garden. In the garden, near the roadway stood a small Egyptian boy. He was so cute that tourists were approaching him eager to give him something. As we neared the boy, someone had given him one Egyptian pound. The young boy yelled to them, "No! Two!" So no one else gave the boy anything .When we left the temple we returned to our ship, had lunch and went on a bus outing to the Great Aswan High Dam, completed in 1970 by Egypt and Russia. As we entered the bus, our driver, a dark Egyptian, did a double take and said to Jim and I, "My family." En route to the High dam the City of Nubia was pointed out to us and we were shown where the city was originally located before it was displaced by the High Dam.

About the Nile River: It's the longest river in the world and on either side, which is seldom more than 12 miles wide, stretches the desert. The Nile is the only river that flows upstream. For thousands of years Egyptians depended on their survival from the Nile's annual flood in late summer, floods caused by spring rains some 1500 miles south in the mountains of Ethiopia. These floods regularly spread a thick layer of rich, black mud over the riverside fields, keeping the hungry desert at bay. But sometimes the floods did not come and Egypt would suffer a famine. Other times the floods were so furious that crops and livestock and even villages were swept away. But now the river has been tamed, thanks to the High Dam.

When we left the High Dam our bus took us to a ferry which took us to Philae Temple. Then back on the bus to the Cataract Hotel where we boarded fellucas, the traditional Egyptian riverboat with a triangular sail, and gracefully sailed back to our ship. Our felluca boatman sang to us and we sang to him. It was a marvelous Sunday afternoon. After dinner, after dark we were taken back to Philae for the sound and light show. I found the show too theatrical, too Hollywoodish.

On Monday, September 28, we visited the famous Abu Simbel Temple via plane and were awed at the size of the statues and the fact that this temple, as was the temple at Philae, had been moved from its original place years ago, piece by piece, for they would have been inundated by the building of the High Dam.

On Tuesday, September 29, we disembarked from our ship and flew back to Cairo where we transferred to a bus which took us along the desert road to the Sheraton Hotel in Alexandria, on the Mediterranean. All those years of geography. The Mediterranean? What? Where? And here I was, right on the Mediterranean.Until we reached Alexandria, Egypt's chief port and second city, 135 miles from Cairo, each day had been hot sun and clear, blue skies But Alexandria had hot sun with gorgeous clouds in the sky. We were told that in most of Egypt it rains maybe once every five years, and then only for two or three minutes. The desert, the desert!!

On Wednesday, September 30, we were given a half day city tour of Alexandria, which seemed very much like a European city. And there were familiar things like Pizza Hut, Wimpy, Kentucky Fried, Pepsi and Coca Cola signs and huge billboards for Brothers Sewing Machine, Mazdas and Sharp Computers. There were also Esso stations and Mobile Mart Service Stations.

On Thursday, October 1, another half day tour included a look at the Royal Jewels and a walk around the grounds of King Farouk's Palace and Gardens, right across the street from the Sheraton. The outside of the palace (we weren't allowed inside) was very impressive in it's opulence. Imagine your initials tiled into each outside corner of the palace. Imagine a passageway built underground from the palace to the beach so that no one could see the big fat Farouk in his bathing suit. The gardens were extraordinarily beautiful. The elevator at the Sheraton showed that the Roof Club and Bar were located on the 36th floor. Yet, our hotel was only 15 stories high.

One evening a dish at the buffet table at the Sheraton was marked "pidgeon." No, I did not touch it.

On Friday October 2, we were transferred after breakfast back to Hotel Mena House in Cairo, but this time we were housed in the modern building next door to where we stayed initially. Our trip back from Alexandria was along the Delta road where I did see some modern farm equipment. We rode through many villages that had what looked to be unfinished houses, only to learn that each hut was ingeniously designed to allow the prevailing north wind to blow through during the desperate summer heat. The flat roofs were covered with animal fodder, laid out to dry, looking like brown, tangled cornsilk. Goats, donkeys and brown-skinned infants filled the narrow thoroughfares seemingly decorated with washing. And water buffaloes were seen here and there.

On Saturday, October 3, we were given a city tour of Cairo. Our first stop was at the Egyptian Museum. On the day we visited the Valley of the Kings a sign over the entrance to the Tomb of Tutankhamun read, "Closed for renovation." But at the museum we saw all the Treasures of Tutankhamun, the child pharaoh who ruled Egypt more than 3270 years ago. The treasures consisted of items found buried in his tomb with his body, items believed to be for his use after death. They were overwhelmingly extravagant, simply mind-boggling; items made of wood, gilded wood, ebony, ivory, alabaster, gold, silver, glass, gold inlaid, quartz, papyrus, lapis lazuli, bronze and copper.

We next went to the pyramids, all different sizes, bewildering in the fact that they're just stones laid on top of stones and they're still standing after all these years. Halfway up the winding road to the pyramids our driver stopped to afford those to alight the bus who chose to ride a camel the rest of the way. My choice was to stay on the bus to the end of the road and shoot pictures of the brave ones riding the filthy-looking camels as they reached us. The hucksters were all over the place, making it very difficult to take a photograph.

Our next stop was at the Sphinx; half man, half lion, sitting there with its broken nose, looking so regal in the late afternoon shadow. That evening we dined at a fancy restaurant in our hotel. Everyone dressed up. We were treated to a show with loud music and gorgeous belly dancers. The food was excellent but if you ordered nothing to drink, you got nothing to drink.

Before going to the dinner show, Tim had us all meet him in an empty lounge to give us papers we would need for our departure. And there, seated among us, were the folks from Quebec, now on their way back home. The shy, young wife gave me such a big smile and hello that one would have thought we were long, lost friends. They left early that evening.

Sunday, October 4, our last full day in Egypt, we did our shopping right in our hotel, as recommended by Tim. For my birthday Jim gave me a gold cartouche bearing my name in hieroglyphics, with a gold neck chain and earrings to match. We purchased a couple of silver cartouches for friends, with their names, a couple of scarab (beetle-shaped) necklaces, and T-Shirts for the grandchildren with their names also written in hieroglyphics. The owner of the shop designed a papyrus with my name and Jim's name in separate cartouches with an anhk in between. The papyrus reads, "Compliments of Old Mena Shop Mohammed Khattab." It's hanging on my travel wall.

On October 5, after a very early breakfast, we were transported to Cairo Airport for our flight to Paris where we had a two-hour wait-over at DeGaulle Airport; where it was a mere 48 degrees and overcast. We almost froze. At the airport we had to go through a security check, our plane was cleaned and we took on a brand new crew. I had a sweet tooth but we only had American money and a few Egyptian coins. There was a Major Polvny and his wife in our group who seemed somewhat distant through the trip. But the Major gave Jim French Francs enough to buy me a Mars Bar. Jim tried to reimburse him in American money, but he refused it.

We were allowed to leave the security area in the airport but had to prove ourselves when we returned. So I went to the area where all the shops were. What a sight! Beautiful shops, beautiful people. I ventured into a perfume shop to purchase an item that cannot be found in New York, but to no avail. It was exciting though, just to be in the packed shop and being surrounded by all that French.

What did I learn about Egypt? I learned that there are 16 million people in Cairo, the largest city in Africa and the largest Islamic city in the world; that there's high unemployment but nobody is starving; that Egypt is 94% desert and 6% farmland; that they grow cotton in the north and sugar in the south; that they also grow maize, rice and clover; that all villages have electricity and running water, even the mud houses; that there are no tributaries off the Nile River but they have an extensive canal system; that a man can marry up to four wives, with the approval of wife #1, as long as he can afford them and be fair and equal to each one; that divorce is not common; that there's a low rate of heart disease and psychiatric illness; that Egypt has a hand-powered economy, which was evident wherever we traveled. I noticed men sitting on the sidewalk fixing the sidewalk with their bare hands; men carrying cement and moving dirt and broken rocks in baskets, and that on a huge road-building project there was little, if any, machinery or heavy-duty equipment. Even so, no scraps of any kind are wasted in Egypt; they find a use for everything.

Ninety per cent of Egypt's population is Muslim. Islam is the state religion. It is acknowledged by the Constitution. Islam is always and everywhere in evidence. It is far more than just a system of belief; it is a code of conduct that regulates every aspect of life; an everyday affirmation of faith.

The majority of Cairo's minarets have balconies from which the muezzin (crier) summons the Muslim faithful to prayer five times daily from mosques all over the city. The call to prayer rings out, as it has done for 13 centuries. (Many of the minarets now have loudspeakers.) It is a moving and beautiful sound, quite different from the church bells that fulfill the same function in Christian countries.

The word "Islam" means simply "submission"-- that is, submission to the will of God (Allah). In practice, Muslims accept as the basis of their public and private life the teachings of the Koran, the book recording the holy doctrine. The very poor in Cairo seem to have solved their housing problem. They are everywhere, squatting in ancient tombs and mosques; taking over derelict houseboats on the Nile. Entire families sometimes live in the "Cities of the Dead" for years. An interesting note: Houses in Egypt were made of perishable stuff but tombs were built to last.

Tim said good-bye to us in Cairo early morning on October 5. He gave each of us a bookmark, thanked us for being "a most splendid bunch," and off he went to meet his next incoming group. When we landed at Kennedy and everyone went their separate way, it was the end of a terrific journey with a beautiful bunch of traveling professionals, all retired and most of whom had been in the educational field.

* * *

EPILOGUE: Tim had compiled a list of our names and addresses, made copies and distributed the list to all of us. We later sent photographs that we had taken of different individuals. This started a chain. We have since received photos they had taken of us, along with lovely little notes. The friendships continue.

Cairo suffered an earthquake two weeks after our return to the States. We have since heard from Tim and he's okay. He was to come to New York to visit us, but tourism is almost at a standstill in Egypt these days and Tim may not even have a job at this point. He owes us a letter.

SPARKS FROM THE CHIMNEY

On September 12, 1929, in the town of Plymouth, N. C., Nettie, age 16, gave birth to a daughter and named her Eleanor.

Louis, my father, married Nettie upon learning of her pregnancy and they lived together in Nettie's mother's home which housed her mother; a married sister, the sister's husband and five children; an unmarried sister, an unmarried brother; and two nieces-- one each from a sister and a brother in New York.

I'm told that shortly after my birth Nettie began neglecting me so my father carried me to his mother, Maggie, who resided a few blocks away; where I spent a night here, a night there. At the approximate age of two years Nettie realized that most of my clothing no longer occupied their usual space in her house, and my presence there, as well as my father's, grew less and less.

Nettie never complained. She made no demands on my father to return me to her. She never visited me. But once in a while my father took me to her house for a visit.

In the house where I lived there was my grandmother Maggie, whom I called, "Mama;" my grandfather Tom, whom I called "Papa;" my father's youngest brother Percy, whom I called "PJ;" and Shockey, the dog. My father and his two other brothers, Aronius and Thomas, moved up north seeking employment. And their only sister, Lillian, was away at school.

Mama and papa's house stood up a narrow lane in a community wedged between two sets of railroad tracks, with dirt roads and no street lights.

The clapboard house consisted of a kitchen, a bedroom, a front room (now called a living room, but back then called a front room no matter in what section of the house it was located), and a front and back porch. The center portion of the house sat on tall, square, red, brick posts, allowing crawl space, but both porches pitched low to the ground.

Shockey, an ugly, greyish, shaggy mutt with hair growing over his eyes, claimed the area underneath the house as his territory. Whenever I left the house he usually remained home with mama. But if mama and I left home together, usually to attend Sunday service at the Methodist church, he would follow us into church and lay under mama's pew, the third pew from the pulpit. And if someone chased him from there, we found him, after church, laying under a pew way in the back of the church.

Nettie was a Baptist, but to my knowledge she seldom went to church during those years.

A broad, flat-top, wood-burning stove occupied a good portion of one end of the kitchen at mama's house; and a small, streamlined pot-bellied wood-burning stove sat in the middle of the front room.

It seemed that whenever we made a fire in the stove in the front room and I went outside after dark either to get more wood from beside the house, or went to the outhouse, which was in the backyard, I always saw Sparks From The Chimney. And I lived in fear that the dry, wooden shingles on the roof might catch fire and burn the house down with mama and me in it. The town's one fire truck did not come to our neighborhood.

Nettie never came to visit.

The lane was shared with two other houses. And at the very end of the lane lay a small, private grave yard. According to my father, when he was a mere lad, one pitch-black, moonless night while his sister sat in the outhouse with the door open, Aronius, my father's oldest brother, threw a white sheet over his head and slowly walked past the outhouse with his hands behind his back and in a loud voice said, "I sure wish I could find my grave." As the story goes, Sis, which is what they called her, bolted from her seat and scrambled into the house screaming.

When papa was still alive we owned chickens and hogs, a big garden and loads of fruit trees, and grew enough for the family and the neighbors. We purchased milk from a neighbor with cows, and flour from the grocery store about a half-mile away. Our trees bore apples, pears, peaches, plums, mulberries, black walnuts and pecans. We also had fig bushes, grapevines, strawberries and black berries. Our garden was filled with white potatoes, sweet potatoes, tomatoes, stringbeans, collard greens, cabbages, turnips, rutabagas, peanuts, squash, canteloups, watermelons, cucumbers, beets, kale and corn. Our flowers were lilacs, roses, violets and hydrangeas. And there was a chinaberry shade tree.

In an effort to demonstrate how helpful I could be to papa in the garden one day, I walked directly behind him and gathered up all these tiny little plants laying like soldiers in a row. How was I to know that papa was dropping the seedlings planning to return, make a hole in the dirt and plant them!

Nettie never came to visit.

Many evenings I was allowed to lie down in bed with papa and I went to sleep in his arms. Next morning I awakened on thc cot in the front room where I always slept. It was fun to get in bed with papa. During one of these times while I was crawling all over him I came upon something long and hard. When I asked him what it was he told me I'd learn all about that when I grew up, but that I shouldn't mention our conversation to mama. I never did. Papa died when I was seven years old.

Nettie never came to visit.

The house directly in front of ours overflowed with children. Their father often came home drunk in broad daylight. And from our front porch I would see him pull his wife to the bed and see them tumbling around on the bed, and I heard strange sounds emanating from both of them. I was not allowed to go to this house, and their children were not allowed to come to mine. Mama, a God-fearing woman who said her prayers every morning and every night and went to church every Sunday, never used a curse word; and the same cannot be said about the family across the way. But I do remember tossing around on the ground a few summer evenings with the boys from that house. It would always be just beyond the two houses and the boys would take turns sticking their penis to the front of my clothing in the area of my private parts; and I liked the way it made me feel. But each time it happened mama soon called to me that it was time to come into the house.

A few years later Professor H. invited me to come to his home with a promise that he would give me piano lessons. I was singing in a trio at school and truly was interested in learning to play the piano. At the very first lesson he tried to hug and kiss me and I got so upset that I threatened to tell Nettie, especially since they were distantly related. He quickly reached into his pocket and gave me pocket change. I never went to his house again; nor did I tell Nettie or anyone else, till now.

Mama washed our clothes every Monday. She made a fire under the big black iron pot out in the yard, where she boiled all the white clothes. The water came from a pump that was situated down a path from the back porch, which meant it was necessary to carry water to the iron pot. Two tin tubs that sat on a shelf just off the porch also had to be filled. If it rained the week before it saved us from having to pump and carry a lot of water; just the tubs had to be moved in place that had caught the rain water in which mama preferred to wash the clothes. When the white clothes finished boiling mama dumped them into a tub of clear water to be rinsed, wrung out by hand, then dumped in a second tub of bluing water for the final rinse, wrung out again and then hung on the lines in the yard. The colored clothes, instead of being boiled, got scrubbed by hand on a washboard, where your knuckles got scraped in the process.

Nettie never came to visit.

At hog-killing time every part of the hog became important. I vaguely remember some of the fat pieces being liquified and mixed with lye and who-knows-what-else. And as this mixture cooled down it became a solid mass of ugliness that eventually was cut into thick bars of soap that was used for scrubbing heavily soiled work clothes. There's an expression, "Ugly as homemade soap." I know exactly what it means.

One wash day, which I later realized had to be Monday, December 8, 1941, I came home from school and mama seemed preoccupied.

I recall President Roosevelt's voice on our old radio saying something about war being declared because of the bombing of Pearl Harbor the day before by the Japanese. And mama became very concerned that P.J., still home with us, might have to go to war. I can remember being very scared and feeling sorry for all the people who lost their lives at Pearl Harbor.

Nettie never came to visit.

Mama and I spent most of our time in the kitchen; a spacious rectangular room with pretty curtains and walls papered with the funnies from the Sunday newspaper to help keep out the drafts from the weather. I never heard of wallpaper until I arrived in New York in May of 1942.

There was no bathroom. Each morning mama heated water on the kitchen stove and poured it into a heavy, baked pitcher and each person, when they were ready to wash up, carried it to a large commode bowl almost as large as a small sink, into the bedroom for privacy. Custom called for taking a bath on Saturday nights. On those occasions a lot more water would be heated and poured into a galvanized washtub setting in the middle of the kitchen floor and one actually sat in the tub and took a bath.

The family never owned a car. But I always had a bicycle. Since the roads lacked being paved on our side of the tracks, I never learned to roller skate. But I still remember the exhilaration of the wind hitting my face while speeding on my bike. For a short time one day I traded my bike for a boy's scooter. And while trying to show off I fell and the scooter tore into my left knee. When I first looked at the deep cut I saw white gristle. Afterwards came the gushing of blood. I wear that scar to this day.

My menstrual period began at age eleven. In those days nobody discussed such things, especially before it occurred. I ran to mama and showed her my bloomers full of blood. She claimed this was normal to happen to a young girl and she proceeded to tear up some old clean bed sheets and fold them; gave me two huge safety pins and showed me how to wear the folded rag inside my bloomers. And when one of these homemade napkins became fully soiled I put on a fresh one but had to wash the soiled one. Nettie never came to visit.

Of the two railroad tracks that wedged the community the short branch went to the box mill and the longer branch served a great portion of the state. This longer branch accommodated passenger trains and very long freight trains. The summer just before my twelfth birthday mama allowed me to meet the passenger trains and sell our huge plums to the passengers. Measuring them in a blue Maxwell House Coffee can, I sold the plums for twenty-five cents a can. The can held seven or eight plums.

A shortcut to school meant walking down the shorter railroad track. Otherwise, we walked what seemed then to be miles through town. On my first return to Plymouth as an adult I realized it wasn't far at all. But during those grammar school days what great fun it was trying to reach the schoolhouse before a train came along. I love freight trains even now. Before P.J. left for the Army I rode my bike down this same railroad track, past the schoolhouse, taking his lunch to him at the box mill during the time school was out (May to August.) I rode to the spot where he worked, usually at a kiln where he fed large sheets of veneer onto rollers that slowly pulled the wood into an oven. And mama always wanted me to bring back a jar of water from the Artesian Well there at the mill. The water always had a faint odor of sulfuric acid, but it tasted real good.

On that same railroad track, in the opposite direction from the school and the box mill, I walked to the ice plant. Our neighborhood received no delivery of ice. One purchased a sizeable piece of ice so that it wouldn't all melt before you walked home. At one point the ice plant hired a black man, the handsomest man I ever saw; with a beautiful brown complexion, dreamy grey eyes, and a smile that would surely light up the heavens. He let Nell and me step inside the freezer one time where they made the ice and it was bone-chilling cold and filled with white vapor and a strange odor.

Nell, my close friend, lived in a big house at the mouth of our lane. What I remember most is the two of us harmonizing Santa

Lucia as we strolled down the train tracks coming from school. I loved visiting her house because there were lots of kids there. On summer evenings we would gather dry cattail plants, dip them in kerosene, stick them in a jar, light them with a match, then sit around the light and tell tall tales or play games or catch lightning bugs and put them in still another jar. Some Saturday evenings there would be an outdoor fish-fry. My introduction to Campbell's Pork and Beans took place at Nell's house. We added lots of ketchup, and they were good.

Going home from Nell's one evening I saw something white down at the end of the lane. Now I don't believe in ghosts and such, but it looked like somebody dressed in white moving towards me. Halfway up the lane, when I could stand it no longer, I yelled for mama and started running towards our house. When I reached the front door mama was there. When I told her why I was so scared, she told me that someone came and whitewashed the huge tree trunk down by the grave yard that afternoon after I left the house.

One beautiful morning, before I grew so tall, I climbed up on the wooden bench on the front porch to take the mail from the mailbox, high up on the wall near the front door. I stood on tiptoes, stretched my arm, lifted the top of the box and reached in. I screamed and snatched my hand away from the box. I felt a sharp pain in one finger on my right hand and frantically shook my hand but the pain didn't go away. I held my hand still for a second and saw a wasp glued to my finger. I screamed louder and began shaking my hand again. Mama came running from around back, caught my hand in midair and extricated the now dead wasp from my finger. Mama theorized that the wasp built a nest inside the mailbox and when I started fumbling for the mail it thought me an enemy destroying its nest. Did you know that when a wasp stings, he plants his needle-sharp stinger into your flesh, lets off a poisonous excretion, and dies? Well, my finger swelled to the size of two and I was frightened and still crying. Mama, trying to calm me down, took me 'round to the back porch where she yelled for Fannie, our nearest and most colorful neighbor in the back, to bring mama some snuff. Fannie not only dipped snuff but she also ate red clay and addressed her son as "Boy"! Mama and Fannie mixed some saliva and snuff, making it into a paste, and smeared it all over the swollen portion of my finger. The swelling gradually receded but I'll never forget the hurt. I'm still afraid of wasps, even though it's said that they won't bother you unless you bother them.

Nettie never came to visit.

During the mid 1930's mama was not privy to the food from the government that some families were allotted. But my maternal grandmother would receive grapefruits, oranges, flour, sugar and hominy (puffed kernels of corn which becomes hominy grits when ground). And if I went over to play with my little cousins on the day the food arrived or a day or so afterwards, I was given a small portion to take home to mama. What stands out mostly in my memory now is the hominy. It was boiled forever until it became soft enough to eat, which unfortunately rendered it tasteless, unless it was seasoned with cracklings; the end product of small, fried pieces of streak-o-lean, streak-o-fat from the hog.The hominy just was not palatable without the cracklings. It was like eating a mouthful of starch. It filled us up though. And many times at Nettie's house there'd be nothing else to eat.

During the late 1930's at mama's house there was never chicken for dinner on the spur of the moment. Mama would need two or three days to pick out the hen that she wanted to kill and separate the hen from the other chickens, purposely not feeding her for those few days. This particular chicken would be confined to a closed coop all by herself. And when the fateful day arrived, mama would take the hen out and literally wring the hen's neck until the neck broke. And the chicken would jump about on the ground for a few minutes before it lay still. When mama grew feeble and couldn't manage to wring the neck, she would cut off the head with an ax. And the hen's body would really jump around then, as if looking for its head. After the blood stopped draining from the chicken, mama dunked the chicken into scalding water so it could be easily plucked of its feathers. Then she washed it and cooked it, usually stewing it with corn and dumplings.

Another dish that we had quite often was dry Northern beans. Mama cooked them with salt pork and a lot of water, resulting in soupy beans, which she served with hot biscuits, small pieces of pork and ice tea with lemon. I didn't even mind sweating as I ate this in the warm kitchen on a hot summer day. No such thing as a cold salad because the weather was too hot; mama cooked every day. Even when there was no food, she cooked. I remember many a meal which consisted of sopping molasses and bacon grease with hot biscuits and with a piece of bacon on the side. And to this day I hate molasses.

There is nothing like ice cream; the best thing to eat in the whole world. Before the war, when PJ came home in what I then perceived as the wee hours, he always brought ice cream for me and mama. No matter what time he reached the house, we gladly got out of bed to eat ice cream. After all, it wouldn't keep in the ice box. I had a little ritual. I'd scrape at the ice cream in my bowl gently with my spoon, making sure I didn't get too much in the spoon, because I wanted it to last forever. Mama would finish eating hers and say, "Sugarbaby, can I have a little bit of yours?" And I would share mine with her. But after this happened a couple of times, I ate mine at the same pace as mama did. Not that I was selfish, mind you; I just loved ice cream. And I still do.

Maybe twice a year mama made ice cream. We each had our stint at turning the handle on the freezer. And of course I always got to scrape and lick the dash. On one such occasion I licked the dash and uttered a loud moan. The ice cream had perfect texture, but it was salty. The salt used on the ice in the process of freezing the fresh cream must have somehow seeped into the container that held the cream mixture. We both sat down and cried.

Nettie never came to visit.

Mama was so industrious. From our peaches she made preserves, from our pears she made preserves, and from our watermelon rinds and cucumbers she made sweet pickles. Our vegetables she chopped together and made sweet relish. This was called chow chow. She boiled the hog head and chopped the meat, filling it with spices, especially sage, and allowed it to congeal into a gelatin-type texture that could be sliced; and this was called souse. From clabber (that's when the fresh cream separated from the milk) she made clabber pudding, adding sugar and flavoring and baking it in the oven with the baking dish setting in a pan of water.

Each year, a week before Christmas, mama began to bake for the holidays. And she stored these delicious morsels in an empty trunk that sat in the kitchen. All the rest of the year the trunk served as an extra place to sit down in the kitchen. But nobody sat on it when it was filled with mama's goodies. She made chocolate layer cake topped with black walnuts; fruit cake, coconut cake, pineapple cake and sweet potato pies. And as her helper, my job was to scrape the bowls and lick the spoons before dunking them into the dishpan and washing them. Christmas meant a slice of all these desserts after dinner, plus a stocking stuffed with a large candy cane, fruit and nuts, and a white doll.

Speaking of white dolls, for two summers in a row mama shipped me off to Aunt Ida (papa's sister) in Elizabeth City, N. C. I travelled by train, me and my big white doll, in the care of the conductor. I thought this quite a long journey. When I grew up I realized that Elizabeth City is only thirty miles from Plymouth. I liked Aunt Ida, even if her house smelled like an icebox full of rancid butter.

Henry Thatch, mama's cousin, who also lived in Plymouth, looked after mama and me after PJ left for the service. He brought us wood as well as food whenever he could. Don't know what would have happened to us without Henry. He invited us to his house one Thanksgiving and he had baked a whole ham, the most delicious ham I ever tasted, also the prettiest; all scored and browned and glazed, with pineapple rings and cherries.

Nettie never came to visit.

I must mention the birds. Several times a year a flock of birds flew to a particular tree in a neighbor's yard that could be observed from our back porch. They would make a lot of noise. Noise, not singing. The noise would stop and only one bird could be heard. Then two or three more could be heard. A few minutes later they could all be heard again and then they would all fly away. Can it be that they were holding a meeting to decide when and where to fly?

One day a big, black, shiny car pulled up in front of our house, relatives of papa's from Texas. When they got ready to leave someone asked me if I wanted to go to Texas with them, and I said yes. So they told me to go pack my suitcase and come along. As I went running into the house to start packing, mama caught me and said, "Sugarbaby, would you really leave me?"

As a child, when a thunder storm came up while I was at Nettie's house everyone laid down and took a nap until the storm blew over. All the kids napped on the floor. On one such occasion I awakened when a rat ran across my face. It left a little bloody scratch on my nose.

A bunch of us kids were playing in an old abandoned woodshed at Nettie's one day and I fell on a rusty nail. It went into the side of my nose, narrowly missing puncturing my left eye. Another time Nettie was in the kitchen at the same house making peanut candy at the stove and we kids were running in and out of the two kitchen doors. My cousin Vivvie ran into my mother as she was removing the frying pan from the stove and the hot candy spilled onto Vivvie's face. To this day Vivvie has a burn mark on her forehead and on her right cheek. She's very attractive though, even with these marks. She's very vain, too-- thinks she's gorgeous.

Nettie never came to visit.

Whenever I went for a visit at Nettie's she always looked me over and sometimes re-combed my hair, but that was it.

One day the children's game turned into rock-throwing. I threw a rock that found its mark on cousin DD's head. When DD screamed and cried out that I had thrown the rock, Nettie sat on the front porch next to me, pulled up my dress and slapped me on my thigh a few times, scolding me at the same time. I recall one other thigh slapping, but can't remember what it was for.

The "Sanctified" Church was down the street from where Nettie lived. The one-room church had no bell. Instead, a little old man stood in back of the church and gave out with a long, loud holler when it was almost time for a particular service to begin. He faced the direction of where most of the members of the church resided, which was all the way across town in an area that was called White City; the color denoting the houses only, for almost all the people living in White City at the time were black. We rarely visited this particular church, but from Nettie's house we could hear the loud preaching, the musical instruments, the singing and the shouting. They always had at least a drum, a tambourine, a piano and a guitar. During what was called revivals at the church we sneaked into the church and stayed at the back, hoping no one would chase us out. And we were mesmerized by the music, the shouting and the dancing in the church. It was quite a show for me, especially having only attended mama's staid Methodist Church all my young life. Incidentally, this "human bell" could be heard all over Plymouth, population approximately 2461 in 1940, as well as what we called "out in the country."

The most colorful character in my neighborhood was Miss Judy Mae (at least that's what we called her). She looked white and she lived alone in a thatched hut on our side of the shorter railroad, and she never spoke to or bothered with anyone in the neighborhood. She wore patches all over her many skirts; colorful patches, patches of all shapes, dirty patches sewn onto her dirty skirts, her multiple dirty skirts, long dirty skirts. It was hard to tell if she was that fat or if she looked fat because of all those skirts she wore at the same time. Her skin even looked dirty; her dirty, white skin. We kids used to laugh at her, but she just ignored us.

Of course there was no television in those days. We had an old radio but the strongest station we could get was the broadcast of the Grand Ole Opry on Saturday nights. My favorite way of entertaining myself at mama's house was to bang on my little toy piano and sing along at the same time.

Nettie never came to visit.

While in grammar school I sang second soprano in an all-girl trio. Mae Etta was the soprano and Catherine the alto. Our theme song was Drink To Me Only With Thine Eyes. We sang it at school and at churches all over town.

There were several teachers from my childhood who left lasting impressions, but two of them really stand out. One was Mrs. Hannah Ballard, who taught kindergarten in her home because there was no kindergarten class at the black public school. The other one was Mr. Walker, my seventh grade teacher, my last teacher before I moved away from Plymouth. He was my sternest teacher ever, and he taught from his wheelchair.

His wife, also stern, and who taught in the same school, pushed him to school each day. When they reached the front steps of the schoolhouse she held his chair while he, bent over, would sort of crawl up the steps holding onto the side wall. Someone always helped his wife bring the chair up the steps and Mr. Walker would sit in the chair and wheel himself into his classroom. Whenever he had to go to the men's room, a male student or teacher would clear the men's room because Mrs. Walker would have to go in to assist Mr. Walker. Her expression was always one of a dutiful wife even though she seemed much younger than he.

While in his class he always mentioned the fact that when his students moved away from Plymouth some of them would write to him, and how this pleased him no end. So when I moved away I wrote to him and we were pen pals for a long while. The relationship came to an end when a telegram came from his wife informing me of his death. I had received a letter from Mr. Walker the day before.

At some point during my early childhood my father moved to New York, divorced my mother, who remained in Plymouth, and took another wife. Soon afterwards I became the best dressed little black girl in all of Plymouth because my Stepmother Bea sent me the cutiest clothes from New York. I know I was the envy of many of my peers. Among my three favorite outfits was an Easter package consisting of a baby blue flared skirt and bolero jacket with a blue blouse with white polka dots, and a natural straw hat with a blue polka dot hatband; a Christmas package consisting of a maroon velvet suit with a white blouse; and a cotton school dress with bold stripes of red, white and blue, with a white collar, and a pair of brown oxfords. I am told that one of my classmates wrote to her mother in New York describing my clothes so that her mother could send the same things to her.

Nettie never came to visit.

Papa had another sister who lived right in Plymouth, Aunt Annie. She was "in the Lord," so to speak, and she sort of stayed to herself. I remember when papa died Aunt Annie yelled out at his funeral, "Lord, my only brother is gone," while her other brother was sitting right next to her. She always walked along the street talking to herself, out loud.

When mama died in March of 1942 my father gave me the option of staying in Plymouth with Nettie or joining him and my stepmother. I chose New York, but I couldn't leave until school closed in May. For the first time in my life I lived in the same house as Nettie. In the interim before leaving Plymouth my father sent my allowance directly to me. I always said that when I grew up and had my own money I would eat all the ice cream I wanted. So with this money in my hands I tried eating ice cream for breakfast. I became so ill that I almost lost my taste for ice cream entirely. Not really. I just never ate it for breakfast anymore.

Back then, there was no such thing as eating out, in a restaurant, at least not for black people. We weren't allowed. And at the Greyhound Bus Station there were two entrances, one in front marked "White" and one in back marked "Colored." There were two separate public water fountains. And at soda counters in drugstores blacks could order anything they wanted but had to take it outside to consume it. There was one movie house in Plymouth. Blacks were only allowed to sit in the balcony.

Some time after 1942 Bea went south from New York to visit her home town of Williamston, N. C., some 20 miles from Plymouth. My father and I remained in New York. While Bea was in N.C. she paid a visit to my Aunt Minerva in Plymouth, who now lived in the same house as Nettie. Minerva and Bea became friends years before when Minerva resided in New York.

I learned, after the fact, that when Nettie and Bea came face-to-face on the day of Bea's visit, Nettie accosted Bea, ripped off Bea's blouse, and accused Bea of stealing Nettie's husband in addition to her daughter.

On hearing of this incident I concluded that Nettie finally came to the realization that she loved me, but that she had lost me to another woman,Maggie notwithstanding. After the incident she began to write to me in New York, nice letters, beautiful handwriting, and signed, "Love, mother."

A teenager now, adjusting to life in New York with my father and Bea, and missing my grandma Maggie terribly, I looked forward to Nettie's letters. And even though she never attempted to take me away from Maggie, even though she never visited where I lived, even though she never seemed to care about me, I saw her in a new light; saw her as the woman I was forever bound to through birth.

Years later, after I married and Nettie remarried, and when it was necessary for me to have a major operation, Nettie came to New York and stayed with me for the first two weeks of my recuperative period. While she was with me I became aware for the first time that Nettie was very shy, to the point of acting subservient even to me.

My heart went out to her. Her letters did the job, as well as her natural demeanor. I became filled with daughterly love. I even took my NewYork-born husband to visit her in little old Plymouth. After that I visited each Mother's Day and at Christmastime.

In the 12th year of my first marriage my husband was well on his way to alcoholism. While I struggled through his loss of a Federal job, his loss of ambition, and his loss of dignity, every few months I received a telegram from Nettie requesting $20 because she and her husband were delinquent in their rent payments and if they didn't pay the money they would be put out on the street. I periodically sent money to her anyway but these were emergency requests, which I honored. That is, until on one Mother's Day visit I observed that her husband was always drunk and she was drinking along with him. Consequently, I stopped sending her money at any time, especially when she sent a request by telegram. I complained to my father that I was in New York struggling to meet my own obligations without help from my alcoholic husband and I refused to send my hard-earned money to Nettie and her husband for them to drink up. So for the period of one year not only didn't I visit, but neither did I send money or even write.

One day, while discussing this with my father, he looked me in the eye and said, "She's still your mother." I considered that statement for about a month and then resumed sending money to Nettie, knowing that what she did with the money was not within my control. Besides, my husband died in 1965 and I was in a better frame of mind.

I also resumed my Mother's Day visits to Nettie, and each time she and Clyde had moved to still another run-down house and their living conditions were pretty bad. At one point I investigated the feasibility of purchasing a mobile home for them, and six months later, in 1977, Nettie and Clyde became the proud tenants of a total electric, two-bedroom, underpinned mobile home within the city limits of Plymouth. I held the title to the two acres of land and the mobile home. Nettie was the happiest and the most grateful woman in the world. Until July, 1978, when Clyde died. My second husband died in October of the same year. And that year Nettie and I became close friends.

Although she was a proud, simple woman and a high school graduate, she spent most of her adult life in service to a Jewish family, raising their two daughters. Her pock-marked, pleasant face sparkled with bright, clear eyes, like the eyes of some birds I've seen. Only five feet tall, and in later years a size 18 - ½ renown for her tiny, cute feet, pretty legs and unforgettable strut; her carriage exuded dignity and pride.

In December, 1983, being diagnosed as having terminal cancer of the stomach, and given a prediction of only two years to live, she accepted the news bravely.

When I first went down to Plymouth to be with her as she was hospitalized, one day she stared at me and said, "I can't believe that you're really MY daughter; you're so pretty and you're so smart!"

Our last month together ended in March of 1984, when she died.

* * *

9/16/92

OBSERVATIONS

The service is scheduled for 1 p.m. Tuesday, January 12, 1993. We arrive at 12 noon. The cathedral is half full. I'm with Richard, a past president of the United Nations Jazz Society. Jim is parking the car. I stop at the third row just before the center of the church and hold three seats off the center aisle. Richard walks down front to see if there are vacant seats. He returns immediately, announcing that there are single seats here and there but no three together. We sit, holding a seat for Jim. A few minutes later I look up just in time to see Jim walking past us. I call to him and ask "Where did you park?" "Right in front," he tells us, "in the special parking section." Luck like this only happens to Jim. His distinguished looks plus his old court badge still work for him. The time passes fast. People flow into the great edifice with the beautiful blue-tinged stained glass windows. It's 12:30 now and all the seats are filled. A crowd forms on both outer aisles just off center and way in the back-- standing room only. People constantly parade up and down searching for seats; familiar musicians, old timers, young people, blacks, whites, people with babies or tiny tots, people with briefcases, cameras, musical instruments, students carrying books, women dripping in mink, women with pretty hats, fine women strutting up and down, back and forth, making sure they are seen. Several musicians stop to say hello to Richard and Jim. An entire class of school children file in and walk all the way down front. Space must have been reserved for them because they do not return.

At approximately 12:50 a musical prelude begins. At about 1:12 the prelude ends. Complete silence! There's movement on our right. Those in the procession make their way to the rear center aisle. The silence continues. Five thousand people, plus.

A lone drum beat is heard. After a few beats a solemn, lone trumpet is heard. Other trumpets join in as the procession moves slowly up the center aisle. Tears roll down my cheeks. Young musicians go by playing horns while older musicians (honorary pallbearers) walk behind them. The priests go by, and the candle bearers. Then the children's choir and the cathedral choir; both dressed in red and white robes.

Can't see what's happening up front; can hear most everything though.

Master of Ceremonies Elliot Hoffman reminds us that this service is really a celebration of the life of Dizzy Gillespie in the New Orleans tradition--make a joyful noise; and that unfortunately we have lost the surprise of Dizzy, his resolving a note, his wisecracks and the blowing up of his cheeks.

Mayor Dinkins tells us that Dizzy was sometimes referred to as the eighth wonder of the world and that he was certainly a New York treasure.

Thelonius Monk, Jr. reminds us that Dizzy was America's jazz ambassador to the world. He then reads a letter sent by President-Elect Clinton and his wife.

Bill Cosby sent a message on tape, the bottom line of which was (referring to Dizzy's music) "There won't be anything new, but there will be a lot of things I never heard of."

Milt Hinton and his wife step to the podium and each say a few words, ending with "Straight ahead, Dizzy."

George Shearing tells us that he met Dizzy in 1948 and that they were close friends; that Dizzy would visit he and his wife very often; and that one day Dizzy came by while they were out in the yard and evidently Dizzy made a motion to Shearing's wife not to say anything. Shearing said suddenly he felt a hand on a part of himself reserved for his doctor and the next word he heard was, "Cough!"

Clark Terry plays "Can't Get Started."

Ray Brown tells how he met Dizzy 47 years ago; that Ray came to New York with his bass, went to a club that very night with Hank Jones. As they're sitting there Hank said, "Hey, there's Dizzy." Ray said, "Introduce me to him." Hank did, and told Dizzy how Ray had just come in town and that he was looking for work. Dizzy said, "Yeah, but can you play?" And Ray said, "Yeah." Then Dizzy said, "Be at my house tomorrow night at 7 p.m. - 2040 Seventh Avenue. The other people at the rehearsal at Dizzy's house the next evening were Charlie Parker, Max Roach and Milt Jackson. Ray dubbed Dizzy "A Leader of Musicians."

Milt Jackson recalls that at a time when he had no place to stay he slept on Dizzy's living room couch for three weeks until Lorraine said, "Look, you been here long enough-- you got to go."

The MC informs us that today the New School announced a jazz scholarship in Dizzy Gillespie's name.

Tony Bennett sent a message which said that his family and Dizzy's family lived near each other at one time and they were always popping in at each other's home. One day Dizzy stopped by and Tony wasn't home. His young son answered the door, looked at Dizzy and said, "Who are you?" Dizzy replied, "I'm Dizzy." The boy said, "But who are you?" And again Dizzy said, "I'm Dizzy. So Tony's son said, "Come on in, I'll give you a glass of water."

John Faddis plays "Swing Low, Sweet Cadillac." Afterwards John tells us how Dizzy was a father figure to him.

Paquito D'Rivera pays tribute to Dizzy in Spanish. Jimmy Owens plays the Dizzy composition "Brother King." Jimmy Heath and Tom Flannagan play "I Waited For You."

Chuck Mangione avows how he met Dizzy when he was fourteen years old through Papa Mangione, who said to Dizzy, "You gotta hear my boys." And one day Dizzy let them sit in with the band. And through Dizzy, Chuck got his first gig with Art Blakey. Chuck also tells us how Dizzy would come by their house for spaghetti and that Dizzy passed the word and lots of musicians came by Chuck's parents' home for spaghetti.

Cab Calloway's daughter Chris appears in her father's behalf and tells us that her father's birthday is December 25th and that Christmas was never Christmas until Dizzy's birthday call came through for her father. Then exclaiming, "My father said I had to do this," she holds her arms up and starts clapping, inviting the audience to clap with her, and yelling out "I'll need help with this," she starts singing "Minnie The Moocher." And she gets audience participation! I can't stop laughing.

Father Genzel of St. Peter's Church reads an article on the subject of jazz written by Martin Luther King for the Berlin Jazz Festival years ago. He now introduces Lionel Hampton. I can't see Hamp from where I sit.

Judge James Nelson, Chairman, National Spiritual Assembly USA, speaks in behalf of six million people of the Baha'i faith; people of various colors, the hues of the rainbow; old, young, men, women, a microcosm. He tells us that the Baha'i Book speaks of the oneness of mankind; that Dizzy lived the principles of his faith; that Dizzy overcame celebrity, escaped fame, walking through it as if it wasn't there; and was a living example of the oneness of man. Judge Nelson continues: "We will miss the symphony of his spirit. It saddens us to know that Dizzy can never be duplicated. He really made a big difference." Judge Nelson continues, telling us that during the November 1992 convention, held in New York City, at Carnegie Hall a jazz concert was given in Dizzy's honor, not because he was ill, but just to show how much he was revered.

It's now 4: 15 p.m. and we're leaving, though the service is not quite ended. I shall never forget Dizzy Gillespie nor the Cathedral of St. John the Divine.

* * *

THE LONGEST JOURNEY

It's 7:15 a.m. on Saturday, April 9, 1994 and our taxi is heading for Kennedy Airport. The car radio is loudly tuned to a French speaking broadcast, so I ask where the driver is from. He tells us that he's a native of Guinea but that he went to school in Senegal, Dakar. When I tell him that we once visited Senegal he seems pleased. He turns his head slightly and I see two carved tribal marks on his temple.

Our American Airline flight takes off at 8:05 a.m. and we survive the breakfast of rubber cheese omelet; hard, tasteless cantaloupe, luke warm coffee; and a box lunch consisting of a half sandwich of turkey and cheese and a cookie. We sit in the middle section of the plane, five seats across; all to ourselves.

We arrive in San Francisco a little after 11 a.m., California time. Toy and Gene, Jim's nephew and his wife, meet us at the airport, surprising us with their new car. After picking up supplies in Oakland for their video shop in Vallejo, thirty miles north of San Francisco, where they reside, we eat breakfast; a real breakfast. They seem genuinely glad to see us. The four of us together generate a lot of laughter.

On Sunday, April 10, the four of us go to church, a church we watched being built on several of our visits to Vallejo. Jim videos the service and because the minister remembers Jim we receive a grand tour of the entire building at the end of the service, especially the sections where the minister himself physically helped to construct.

Back at the house we change clothes and drive out to a great seafood restaurant some distance from Vallejo, where we enjoy the food and each other. When we return home we watch cable movies on the movie channel.

Toy makes an exceptionally nice breakfast on Monday, April 11. Then she and I go shopping. I spend the remainder of the day getting our things together for the next leg of our trip.

On April 12th we board a bus at a nearby Holiday Inn which takes us to the Frisco Airport where we take a short plane hop to Los Angeles to catch our Quantas flight to Fiji.

While checking in at the US Air/Quantas counter at the Frisco Airport the ticket agent says she has interchanged our frequent flyer numbers on the computer and she's having difficulty correcting it. With only the two of us waiting on line, a second agent appears from nowhere and engages us in small talk, all the while apologizing for the confusion on the computer. The lady at the computer remains calm but the second agent keeps nervously talking to us and being quite nosey. With only thirty minutes left from our one-hour scheduled departure time, things suddenly become straight and we are released from the counter. As we head for the gate we decide to stop in the restroom. When we come out and as we continue towards the gate, we recognize the nosey lady from the counter walking with a six-foot guy who is speaking on a walkie talkie. She ignores us. I hear the guy say, "False alarm; Morton. False alarm. Black couple." Obviously, Jim did not hear this so I mention it to him as we continue to proceed to the gate. As we sit down in the gate area wondering out loud what is going on, a lady sitting near me leans over and says that the name "James Morton" seemed to be the subject of a police search by "six Rambo- looking cops who were all over the place." She doesn't know what the suspect is wanted for.

As we board our plane to the LA Airport for our hook-up with Quantas, people look at us slyly as we take our seats. Just before take-off, two stewardesses come to Jim and say, "So you're the man the police thought they were after?!" They tell us that the police instructed the pilot to await police clearance before take-off; that everyone was concerned; and that other passengers initially did not want to get on the same plane with us. The stewardesses think Jim deserves a drink, so they bring him two; compliments of the airline. We never find out any details, only that they caught the guy. Even the response to Jim's letter of complaint later to Quantas fails to enlighten us.

We leave LA the same day and arrive at Nadi Airport in the Fiji Islands on Thursday, April 14 at 4 a.m.; having crossed the International Dateline. At the airport a white man with a tour group approaches Jim and asks if he is from Baltimore; that Jim looks just like someone he knows back in Baltimore. Jim extends his hand, saying, "That's all right; it happens to me all the time. Jim Morton's my name." The man extends his hand saying, "I'm Bob" somebody; "Sorry 'bout that."

"Bula" (hello) Friday, April 15. At breakfast, one waitress thinks me an American TV star! We enjoy the tasty banana pancakes, with Karo syrup no less, while sharing the dining room with a group of German tourists and/or businessmen. After breakfast, Peter, our hotel van driver, drives us from our beautiful country setting into town, leaving us on our own for a couple of hours. We visit the craft market and then people-watch along the main street for a while. As we stroll along, three young girls get my attention and say, "Hello." When I answer with a smiling "Hi," I hear them say, "She said "Hi" and they giggle. I have a distinct feeling I'm being mistaken for someone else.

When Peter picks us up he drives to what he refers to as our sister hotel, an ultra modern hotel consisting of apartments only, with a magnificent view of mountainous rain forests and grass-covered hills. Our hotel is okay and is comfortable but the two do not even look like sisters. Peter lets us see an unoccupied duplex apartment with an extra bedroom upstairs, king size beds, a television, a VCR; a breakfast terrace; and in the kitchen we observe a convection oven as well as a microwave oven. The rate at the modern hotel is $190 Fijian dollars per night. Our hotel is $65 Fijian dollars per night. During our stay, one American dollar is worth one dollar and thirty-nine cents in Fijian dollars.

Fiji, a quiet, tropical Third World country consisting of hundreds of islands in the South Pacific, is inhabited by beautiful native Fijians, North Indians, South Indians, birds, frogs and lizards. The country is covered by a gorgeous blue sky and is shrouded in exotic flowers that flourish in the tropical heat. It's a great place for scoober diving or swimming or water skiing or fishing. One is greeted everywhere with a cheerful "Bula" and we quickly learn to say "Finaka" (thank you) at the appropriate time. The traffic moves on the left; and we see no American cars. The weather is so hot, the men wear skirts (sulu's). The police wear white sulu's with a navy uniform top and a white hat.

Fiji seems to be stopped in time because the music we hear is the music that played in the States in the 1950's. The women's hair styles also seem stopped in time. I see no one with braids; women mostly wearing long afros. If a woman wears a flower behind her left ear or on the left side of her head, it means she's single. Worn on the right signifies she's married.

All the rooms in our hotel are located on the ground level. No television, but a frigidaire and facility for making coffee. On Saturday morning Jim serves hot coffee on the patio. I don't know what time it is but it is very, very early. The scene is peaceful and green and the birds are singing away. Suffering from jet lag, we return to bed, skipping breakfast yet. The best part of Fiji is the early morning discussions while sipping coffee on the patio. The worst part is sharing my shower with a little lizard. We travel with our own music and we enjoy that. We accomplish a lot of reading, too; books that we brought with us. In the evening we walk to the thatch-covered bar where we are entertained, along with the other guests, by three or four men dressed in print sulu's, playing guitars and a ukulele; harmonizing old, old songs. Would you believe Waltzing Matilda (Australia's unofficial national anthem)? One day we take a camera-and-video-walk but we don't wander too far because there is no sidewalk where we are and it's so hot. We eat the same thing for dinner each night, turkey, lettuce and tomato on roll and bypass the nightly poolside barbecues to avoid becoming ill in the tropical heat. The sandwich is quite good.

By Tuesday, April 19th we are well rested and more than ready to continue on our Longest Journey. We are up at 4:30 a.m., at the airport at 5:30 a.m. and our plane leaves for Brisbane, Australia, at 7 a.m. We arrive in Brisbane four hours later. A nice flight, with the movie Mrs. Doubtfire.

Who ever thought that a chance meeting on a train might bring an invitation to visit Australia! The sharing of a first class compartment on a train in Europe in the fall of '93 results in just that. What a welcomed change to share a compartment with English speaking travelers! Heather and I, sitting almost side by side, become deeply involved in conversation while Ian, who sits facing his wife, reads his newspaper, sneaking looks at her which seem to say, "She's at it again!" Jim, sitting across from me, busies himself with a magazine. I offer Heather a mint. She accepts and gives me a little kangaroo lapel pin. She has forgotten to pack a shower cap so I dig into my carry-on and give her an unused one from one of the many hotels. Jim and Ian get caught up in our conversation which now turns to how each one earns a living. Ian, a civil engineer/manager of large construction projects, i.e., casinos, golf courses, breweries, carparks, hotels/motels, high rise residentials, commercial and industrial projects in many countries, extends his business card to Jim which indicates that they live in Brisbane, Australia. Jim reads the card and looks at Ian saying, "Now, don't invite us unless you mean it, because we'll show up." All of us laugh it off. Just before the train pulls into Brussels I remember our left-over coins of French francs and give them to Heather as they head for Paris. (Foreign paper money is easily exchanged in most countries and in the US but rarely can you exchange coins.) Then I snap a picture of Heather and Ian. They help us with our luggage from the overhead rack and shake our hands goodbye.

Later, back in the States, my photos of Heather and Ian are so nice, I mail them to Australia. Almost one month later comes a beautiful letter from Heather, including photos of their home and a nearby tourist kangaroo park. A frequent correspondence develops. (Since it takes from seven to ten days for air mail to arrive between NY and Brisbane, the "frequent" means approximately once a month). One of Heather's descriptive letters contains a photo of what she refers to as a "granny flat," which includes the sentence, "This is where our visitors stay-- hint, hint." It shows their custom built home and another little brick house separated from the main house by a patio and a swimming pool.

I remember reading some time ago how some people in foreign countries cope with caring for aging parents by building a small accommodation for the parent adjacent to the children's own home; and that they refer to the dwelling as a granny flat.

By January 1994 Jim begins to bug me about going to Australia to visit Heather and Ian. I don't even want to hear it because it is too far away. One day he asks me under what conditions would I consider making the trip at all. I blurt out, "Only if we stop somewhere on the way and also stop somewhere on our return." He replies, "Okay, map out what you want and I'll give it to our travel agent and see what she comes up with." I propose the following:

1 - NY to Frisco with 3 days in California
2 - LA to Fiji with 2 days in the Fiji Islands
3 - Fiji to Brisbane, Australia, with 7 days in Brisbane
4 - Brisbane to Hawaii with 3 days in Hawaii
5 - Hawaii to LA to Frisco with 3 days in California
6 - California to NY

Meantime, since most people we meet in our travels assume Jim and I to be an old married couple, we figure that Heather and Ian assume the same. So this necessitates a letter of explanation to them as to whether their invitation still holds. A letter comes rushing back to the effect that they almost feel hurt that we even entertain the idea of them being so judgmental or narrow-minded.

Next, we determine what time of the year to visit, since their seasons are just the opposite of ours. Heather suggests April because that's their fall season when the weather is quite pleasant--warm during the day, sweater weather at night.

We choose dates. Then I feel that I want to talk to Heather to hear what she really thinks about us coming and whether our dates suit them and how long to stay, et cetera, et cetera.

What a chore just to figure out when to make the call, because if it's 12 noon on Thursday in NY, it's 3 a.m. Friday in Australia.

I call. In disbelief she accepts the fact that we plan to visit and she is oh so excited. Our dates agree with her as well as our length of stay--strictly up to us. She wants nothing from NY; just us.

After speaking to Heather via phone she sends letters describing our room in the granny flat, describing the beds, the bath and shower and storage space; and the attached office from which they run the business. The office has a TV at our disposal; also a well-stocked refrigerator full of fine wines and beer. The letters also contain brochures and flyers describing different places in Australia that might be of interest to us so we arrive with an idea of what we want to see or do while in Brisbane.

One day Heather calls me specifically to inquire as to whether I use a hair dryer and if so, not to bring mine; that I can use hers because the electrical plugs in Australia differ from ours in the States. Jim needs a travel plug for his razor. (They have 220 triple plugs as compared to our 110 double plugs.)

As our plane from Fiji arrives in Brisbane, Jim says to me, "Are we out of our minds? What are we doing here??!" We see Heather waiting. When she spots us, she beams and welcomes us with open arms. We hug and kiss and hug like long separated friends.

Fifteen minutes later she pulls into her driveway and we are greeted by her 23 year old barefooted son who is instructed by Heather to take our luggage to the granny flat. After unpacking, we are given a grand tour of their beautifully decorated home on a hill in a suburb of Brisbane, overlooking their neighborhood, with a broad, expansive distant view of downtown Brisbane and surrounding mountains. At the end of the tour she presents us with a computer printout of a proposed itinerary for us, covering our entire stay. We look it over.

Previously, via mail, we are informed of the availability of Heather and her car to take us wherever we want to go. She even researches short tours and overnight stays in case we want to break away from the Frankland's; Heather, Ian and Peter. Also, we are informed via mail of Ian's returning home from a business trip in Sydney the evening of our arrival. And when we arrive at the airport, Heather informs us that Ian has called to say he's arriving around 10 p.m. To our surprise, he actually arrives home a little after 8 p.m. from Sydney, three hours flying time to Brisbane. He welcomes us and immediately makes drinks for everyone and we drink a toast to a pleasant stay.

We approve and accept Heather's proposed itinerary and on Wednesday she takes us to the Walkabout where we receive a private lecture on the Platypus (peculiar only to Australia) by the young curator of the museum of natural history and where we see snakes and turtles, etc., and a Platypus in a glass tank together with many diverse types of fish. What high speed antics the Platypus performs, keeping us laughing all the while we try to photographically capture him.

The center of the Walkabout contains a rustic, outdoor restaurant on stilts, high up in the air. I'll always remember our snack of lemon meringue pie and coffee. Pure condensed milk with lemons. Yum yum! As we share the rich pie, Heather spots a Kookaburra (a large bird that makes noise like a laughing jackass) in a nearby tree. Heather, well versed in her native birds and trees and flowers, explains that this particular Kookaburra is searching for food. He sits in the tree for a long, time, turning his head from side to side. We have it all on videotape. On the way back to the car Heather points out a Zingiber (ginger) bush. Peter majored in horticulture in college and he and Heather call all the plants by their formal names.

The top of the picture windows in our room are high up on the wall, near the ceiling. And though the drapes are drawn at night, daylight seeps in underneath the drapes early morning. One morning I hear a slow, deliberate whistle that is really beautiful but makes me feel uneasy. I can't wait to tell Heather at breakfast that I think it to be a man whistling a tune just outside our window. She asks me what the tune was like. When I repeat it as best I can she laughs and replies, "Oh, that's just a Butcher bird!" "A bird, I cried!" Heather said "Yes, they're very melodic." I can't remember whether she mentions that it's a mating call or what, but I find it strangely beautiful each early morn. Heather introduces me to lots of their native birds and plants and trees and flowers. Ask her about any of these and she'll run the whole history down for you, proper names and all. Later in 1994 she mails me a compact disc of Australian birdcalls, which includes several Butcher birdcalls. It's fascinating.

On Thursday she takes us to the Woolshed for lunch and a show. After lunching on luscious lamb, we enter the room where the ram show is about to begin. Heather suggests a suitable spot for Jim to do his videotaping of the sheep as they make their entry and later their exit from the room. She and I sit elsewhere. Six huge, unusual looking sheep, each one different from the other, enter from a side door, turn and walk up the main aisle, past rows of people, take the few steps up to the stage to their assigned places where they are fastened to some sort of stanchion for the duration of the show; all this with the assistance of a sheep dog. The show demonstrates, with a young calf, what happens from the time a sheep is sheared of its wool until the wool is knitted into a garment. The shearing is done to music. Samples of the wool are given to a few members of the audience to feel the natural lanolin the wool contains. A young lady shows how yarn is made and, with a spinning wheel, demonstrates how a sweater is made.

At the end of the show the sheep, unfastened, are to leave the stage, pass the audience, turn, and exit the way they entered. The sheep dog is to keep them in line. But on this day one of the sheep turn in the wrong direction and walk down the row where Jim is videotaping. Jim is the only person in that row. Heather and I hold our breath and helplessly watch Jim. The wayward sheep just struts past Jim and Jim never even flinches. One of the fellows in charge comes running and cussing at the dog and the sheep; grabs the sheep and steers it to the proper exit. It turns out that the sheep dog is new on the job. When we calm down, Heather comments that as many times as she has observed the show (and she's taken so many visitors that the Woolshed has given her a permanent free pass) she's never seen anything like what happened that day.

From the show we walk across the yard to watch other sheep dogs round up herds of sheep. Then on to feed the kangaroos and see the Koalas (we call them Koala bears but they're really not bears). I have a photo made of me holding one. The kangaroos eat their feed right out of your hand. Their long tongues tickle my hand and I can't stop laughing. The koalas are all half asleep in the Eucalyptus trees, their natural habitat, where they get high from eating the leaves.

Friday we beg for a day of rest. Jim and Peter remain home to enjoy the blues cassettes that Jim brought from home, after learning that Peter likes the blues, while I go food shopping with Heather at Woolworths Food Supermarket, not related to our Woolworth Five and Dime Stores. We also buy some Moreton Bay Bugs (seafood-- sort of like lobster) from Heather's favorite fishman parked alongside the road. We stop at a post office so I can get stamps for my cards. Their post offices carry almost everything that our stationery stores carry, but instead of postal windows they have an ordinary counter and a computerized cash register.

One afternoon Heather takes us downtown Brisbane to meet Daphne, Ian's sister, for lunch at an outdoor restaurant called Jimmy's On The Mall. Daphne is a saleslady in a big department store similar to Macy's and she handles the wedding registries, etc. After lunch we shop for opals and visit another department store where one floor is only for children, with an overhead train on a track that rides the children all around that floor.

On that same afternoon we meet Ian and he drives the four of us to Paradise Springs Golf Course, one of his projects. On the way there he points out the Powers Brewery, another of his projects. Then on to Queensland's Gold Coast to the Jupiter Hilton Casino; again, where Ian served as chief engineer and project manager. We snack at the casino but "invest" no money. As we wait in the lobby for Ian to bring the car around for our return home we see a videotape advertisement being continually shown and Ian is seen at work in the video. He is aware of the video but has never seen it himself. He does not see it this day either.

On Saturday Ian drives us to the Big Pineapple and Macadamia Nut Farm. We learn that Macadamia nuts originate in Australia, not Hawaii, as we thought. We see them growing on trees and of course purchase toasted and salted ones at the farm. He then drives us to Mooloolaba and we have lunch at Adonoplay's on the scenic waterfront. I eat Barracundi fish, fried in beer batter. Deelish! From there he drives us to the Glass House Mountains, about which there is an Aboriginal legend; but I will not go into that at this writing. The mountains are ethereal.

On one of our outings Ian wears a navy blue, short-sleeved pullover knit shirt with the logo, "Jupiter Casino-1993." Jim and I both rave about the shirt. So Ian promises to give us shirts when we visit his job site.

Sunday morning Ian takes us to his job site, yes, where he is chief engineer and project manager. We don hard hats and boots for our safety and receive permission to take certain photographs. I receive my promised shirt in white. They are out of the navy one for Jim, but Ian promises to get one from the casino before we leave Brisbane. The site, located in Brisbane's Central Business District and overlooking the Brisbane River, consists of the historic Treasury Building and the adjacent Queens Park and Lands Administration Building. The buildings are being restored and transformed into a casino and a hotel but the facades have to remain the same. A park is located between the two buildings. The park is to be removed in order to build a parking lot underground and then the park is to be placed on top of the parking lot. We trudge through the diggings, the cement and mud in the hollowed-out buildings with Ian proudly describing and explaining what is going on at the moment. In the midst of all the chaos we stop at one door and Ian pulls out keys from his pocket and unlocks the door. We enter into a gorgeous, fully completed, fully decorated guest room. It has a full bath, with a marble floor, a marble sink, marble around the tub and a glass enclosed shower. The room has a very high ceiling and colorful matching drapes and bedspread. Ian asks our opinion as to the furnishings and the placement of the furniture and TV, et cetera, and he marks down our suggestions. He explains that it's what they call a "mock up" room in the industry, just to see how the finished product is going to work.

That same afternoon we celebrate Heather's 55th birthday with a picnic on Mt. Jolly, Heather's longtime wish. Ian and Katie, their grown daughter who lives elsewhere, put everything together and two cars make the trip, loaded with us and food. We have a very beautiful view; only thirty minutes from home. And we refuse to let intermittent rain spoil our fun. But Jim never lets up on Heather about the fact we sit eating in the rain. Katie and Heather cover him with a golf umbrella all the while.

Early evening, the same day, Daphne and Tracy, Daphne's grown daughter, come to the house after work and Ian orders Chinese food (the best I've ever eaten). Rita, Peter's girlfriend comes over, too. The evening turns into a feast, plus birthday gifts, birthday cards and a cake with a candle "singing" Happy Birthday. It all ends with drinks, coffee and cake and Daphne following Jim around the room.

The day before we leave for Hawaii Heather takes us to Mt. Cootha (Aboriginal name meaning "place of wild honey") with a panoramic view of practically the whole of Brisbane. From there she takes us to an Aboriginal gift shop and art museum. The art on exhibit and for sale is fantabulous but way, way beyond our means, even in Australian dollars. (Our dollar is worth $1.19 of their dollar at the time we are there.) The sales help in the gift shop is not Aboriginal. They are black, but are from Torres Strait Island, off the northern coast of Australia. One salesgirl has a boyfriend in the Bronx.

On April 27th Heather drives us to the airport along with Peter. Ian goes to work but promises to meet us at the airport. When he arrives, he hands Jim a package, describing it as a special delivery to his office that very morning. It is the promised blue knit shirt in Jim's size.

An emotional departure it turns out to be, with lots of tight hugs and warm expressions. Shy Ian hugs me and whispers, "It was really nice, Ellie." We insist that they head for home long before our plane is to take off, because we're all getting teary-eyed, all but Peter, that is. He looks sad though, as if he hates to see the "Desperado" leave. (This is the name Peter dubbed Jim after hearing about the incident involving the so-called Rambo cops at the airport in California.) Before they leave us we remind Heather and Ian that they are to visit us at their earliest convenience.

We must fly south to Sydney to get the Quantas flight to Hawaii, which takes us north first, to Cairns, flying back over Brisbane. We leave Cairns around 7:15 p.m. Australia time on April 27th and arrive in Honolulu at 8:30 a.m. Hawaiian time the following morning. And it's still April 27th.

It is such a lovely, warm day that immediately after registering at the Waikiki Beach Hotel, and though I am dragging from lack of sleep (I can't sleep well on a plane), we quickly change into shorts and walk along the beach across the street from the hotel, still taking pictures, of course. I sleep very well that evening.

During the next few days we walk a lot and we take a city tour, visiting the Pearl Harbor Memorial, Dole Cannery Square (a shopping center now but once was the Dole Pineapple factory), Hilo Hattie (a garment factory of tropical prints, gifts, souvenirs and TShirts) and a jewelry design center. We ride a city bus to visit acquaintances who migrated from Brooklyn, N.Y. but now live an hour or more from Honolulu. They are happy to have visitors from New York. We want to take them to dinner, but they insist on taking us. So they drive us back to Honolulu, treat us to dinner at a place called the Yum Yum Tree, and drop us at our hotel before returning to their home. It's a most jovial time.

On the 30th we return to Vallejo, California, and spend three more wonderful days with Toy and Gene. On May 4th we arrive back home in New York and find everything in order.

* * *

EPILOGUE:

Approximately one year later, on Good Friday, April 14, 1995, Heather and Ian come to visit and stay with me in my six-and-a-half-room apartment for eleven days. She has written that she wants to see Central Park, and visit the Frick Collection of Art in New York City; and that Ian is interested in the Smithsonian Institute in Washington and would also like to see a small fishing town.

On Saturday Jim drives us to the Promenade in Brooklyn Heights, then to Manhattan, over the Brooklyn Bridge, and we take the East River Drive, passing by the United Nations Building, continuing on uptown to Harlem. He drives us through Striver's Row, past the

Schomburg Center for Research in Black Culture, pointing out Harlem Hospital; and drives us through 125th Street, pointing out the Apollo Theatre; the works.

On Easter Sunday he drives us to Central Park. Heather, Ian and I walk around a bit and take pictures. Back in the car, Jim drives us down Fifth Avenue. We see the tail end of the Easter Parade. Then we go to the Frick Museum. When we leave the museum, Heather remarks that she doesn't really have to see anything else because she has so thoroughly enjoyed the Frick collection of original art work by the masters, something she has been wanting to see since her college days.

From the museum, Jim takes us past the Empire State Building and down to the World Trade Center. It is so mobbed with people that we don't bother to go up for fear of missing our 6 p.m. dinner reservation at Peter Luger Steak House in Brooklyn. But since we have a little time, Ian asks if he can just take a look in the lobby of the newly renovated Vista Hotel. We walk inside and immediately Ian runs into a man he knows from Australia who turns out to be in charge of the hotel. Ian wants to see behind the scenes but we run out of time. So the man gives Ian his phone number and tells him to call and he will set up a day and time when Ian can return and be shown around the hotel. Ian calls on Monday and an appointment is made for Tuesday at 11 a.m.

Tuesday, after dropping Ian off at the Vista, we take Heather to Barnes and Nobles and Tower Records, returning for Ian a couple hours later. She is in search of the book From Slavery To Freedom, by the historian John Hope Franklin and we can't find a copy. We end up in Nassau County at Borders Books near Fortunoff's where a very helpful salesman locates the book, via telephone, in a nearby mall; reserves it for us and we pick it up. Since we are right at Fortunoff's we take them in and Ian purchases a very nice pen for Heather's upcoming birthday on April 24th.

We have been invited to New Paltz, New York, on Wednesday to visit a winery and to spend the night with an interracial couple. It works out quite well. Early the following morning the six of us, in two cars, drive to Foxwood, the casino in Connecticut, so Ian can compare it with his casino project back in Brisbane. Upon our arrival at the casino Miss Eleanor is instrumental in Ian meeting the manager of the casino and he and Heather are given the grand tour. Ian is even allowed to send a FAX to Brisbane, free of charge, for the opening of the casino there, which is on that very day. In Connecticut we're right near a fishing village but it's dark now and we're exhausted. We four return to New York late that evening.

On Thursday morning the four of us leave for Washington, D.C. with Jim and myself sharing the driving. Our reservation is for two nights. Heather and Ian, on their own during the day to visit the Smithsonian or wherever they choose, meet us for dinner each day. In fact, the first evening, dinner is on a friend of theirs who is in London. The friend is the interior decorator of the swanky Bombay Restaurant in Washington and when he learns that Heather and Ian may visit Washington, he sets up with the owner for the four of us to have dinner there. We dress up for our 8 p.m. dinner. Ian suggests we take a taxi to the restaurant so that Jim can be totally relaxed. Our taxi driver, recognizing Ian and Heather's accent, tells us of the many years he spent in Australia and Heather and Ian become overwhelmed. At the restaurant the red carpet is rolled out for us and we have a splendidly delicious time savoring the many Indian dishes.

We arrive back in New York before dark on Saturday and are glad to be home. I plan an "open house" for Sunday between 12 noon and 4 p.m. for Heather's birthday and invite people from all walks of life so that Heather and Ian can get a well-rounded picture of New York. Twenty-five people show. Thoughtful Heather, not knowing of my plans, because in truth it is a last minute decision on my part, brings a bunch of little kangaroo lapel pins from Australia for me to give to my friends and everyone receives one. People come and go during the four hours and a few linger afterwards. I am well pleased with the day. Heather meets no strangers, so she has a jolly good time. As one of my friends later said about the two of them, "She bubbles; he flows."

On Monday we take them to breakfast at a local soul food restaurant. Our waitress orders Heather, calling her " honey," to take her glasses off the table and put them in her pocketbook, to make room on the crowded booth table. And, listening to our conversation and hearing Heather's accent she asks where Heather is from. Then she proceeds to tell Heather her personal business, i. e. she's retiring soon and moving south and what she's going to do when she retires, and on, and on and on. Heather cuts her eye at me and we try to hold back our laughter. When Jim orders biscuits and Heather is curious, saying she doesn't know what they are, we order extras so Heather can see and taste them. When they arrive heather says, "Oh, they're scones! We call them scones!"

While in Australia, Heather expresses to us that she always wanted to visit New York but she is afraid, especially after seeing the news of New York on television and they don't know anyone in New York. So I promise that now that they know us, when she comes to visit I will not let her out of my sight.

They travel light, so I take her to the laundryroom in my building on thc day after their arrival. On all the further, numerous trips to the laundryroom Ian escorts her. Long after their departure from New York, my neighbors in different sections of the building are saying to me, " Ellie, I met your nice visitors from Australia!" Heather must have told everyone she saw that she was visiting "Ellie Speer."

We know they enjoyed themselves because we enjoyed having them. We are sad to see them leave on Wednesday April 26th, heading for Vancouver Island to spend three days with a friend they have not seen for ten years.

Did I mention that Ian is a native of Ireland and that Heather is a native of Australia and that they met and married while both were working in New Zealand?

They call when they arrive back in Brisbane. They also call the day after the Blizzard of '96 to see if we are okay. And the correspondence responsible for The Longest Journey continues...

* * *

April, 1996

Eleanor Speer
17224 133rd Avenue #7G
Jamaica, NY 11434-3902

(718) 712 6694